MW00860994

MICHAEL S. SMITH HOUSES

Michael S. Smith
Houses

With Christine Pittel

RIZZOLI
NEW YORK

Contents

Introduction

For everybody, it starts the same way. The source of an idea for a room could be a house you visited as a child, but prettier and better than yours. Or a great hotel you stayed in that gave you a whole other experience, maybe a special sensory impression. All those memories and sensations contribute to what you think your ideal house should be, and the images get compounded and more complex as you add some ideas, eliminate others, and move on. So the dream in the dream house shifts and reshapes itself in your mind's eye, depending on the last movie and the next magazine. It's like a cliff that's been eroded and carved by many factors over time.

How does one idea rise to the surface and become a guiding concept? The initial impulse could come from anywhere—something you see on television or glimpse in a book. A particular color combination might catch your eye. Or it could be as simple as seeing a picture of a room in an ad and projecting yourself into it. All of us are influenced by subtle things that are really profound.

I think we collect images. We string them together like beads until we have a rough notion of what our dream house could be. In an issue of *House & Garden* that I must have seen fifteen years ago, there was a room by a decorator who's long gone, Harrison Cultra. He was a genius—talented, talented, talented. On the Victorian parlor floor of a New York brownstone, he did pink walls, stripped pine furniture, overstuffed white cotton duck upholstery, and palm trees. It's something I still carry

around with me as one of the most beautiful rooms I've ever seen. Very unexpected. It's in my mental file, waiting.

I would tell the average person thinking about designing a house to sit down and make a list of what you're really drawn to. What do you like? What are you pursuing? What's in your mental image bank?

In the office, when we're brainstorming a project, I always ask, "What's the movie?" We live in a time when our idea of how we should live is completely altered by the movies, which offer every decorating touchstone in the book. What should this house be? Is it that airy, aristocratic Main Line house from *The Philadelphia Story*? Or is it a New York apartment from *The Eyes of Laura Mars*, a bizarre film that influenced an entire generation of decorators. People are always asking me if I designed that iconic Hamptons house in *Something's Gotta Give*. We all share these indelible images from the movies. They're part of a collective visual unconscious, a pool of references we can draw on.

For relaxation, I go through real estate ads all the time, which is weird, I know. Right now I'm looking at Paris flats, houses in Spain, New York apartments, ranches in Ojai, and beach houses in Laguna. Occasionally I'll be tempted by an inn for sale in East Hampton or a beautiful brick house in Glen Cove. I'll do the math, study the pictures, envision myself in each house. What would life be like if I lived there?

Designing a house is also a bit like the movies because you're making up stories. I'm working on a

---

At first glance, this looks like a casual collection of objects on a table, yet there is a connecting thread. Everything is very sculptural—the smooth lingam stone, a 1930s French starfish carved out of wood, an eighteenth-century copy of a Greco-Roman fragment. Even the vase, bought at the Paris flea market and probably nineteenth-century French, has a very unusual silhouette. The colors are muted and monochromatic. I wanted the eye to linger over texture and shape.

project in Southampton right now, a turn-of-the-century, tile-roofed, vaguely Mediterranean house, and I keep coming back to the idea of Gertrude Vanderbilt's painting studio in Old Westbury. I haven't seen those pictures in ten years, and I might be disappointed if I saw them now. But in my mind's eye, it's a colorful, turn-of-the-century Bohemian interior within a Beaux Arts house. I was looking through a Sotheby's catalogue and saw an ebonized faux-bamboo writing desk—very Herter Brothers, Anglo-Japanese, Aesthetic Movement—and thought, that's it, with a chair in bright turquoise-and-yellow Liberty & Co. linen. So the story is, you're the daughter of William Henry Vanderbilt and have all this Herter Brothers furniture that was made for your family's mansion on Fifth Avenue. But this is the beginning of modernity and you're young and you've put it together differently. It feels new and fresh to me, not a brown Gustav Stickley version of Arts & Crafts but a more organic, vivid James McNeill Whistler, Peacock Room interpretation. I'm having a Liberty moment right now.

We all make our own stories up in our heads, and they become part of the vision. When I'm working with a client, the process is very personal. It's about listening to people and drawing out their thoughts. When clients tell me they want to build a French house, my job and my joy is to reach into my library of mental images and pull out all sorts of options, in an effort to figure out what a French house really means to them. Is it something like the Belle Epoque villa built for Coco Chanel on the Riviera, or more like Yves St. Laurent's apartment in Paris? So much of what any good decorator does is listen. I've become a very good therapist over the years, and I can tell what people really want, which is different than what they think they want.

Then I start to weave all these ideas and images together into something that's unique and complex. I don't paint myself out of the picture. It's not just about the client. Their ideas are filtered through my sensibility.

This room, and everything in it, is big in scale. The ceiling is high and the windows are tall, so I needed some strong verticals to suit the lofty proportions of the space. The steel campaign bed, based on an Italian original and topped with a simple canopy, is unusually tall. The two contemporary works on paper are Japanese brushstroke paintings. The Chinese tables in front of the sofa are made of stone.

It's as if I'm directing a movie that was written by someone else. I have to take their vision and turn it into three-dimensional reality.

I like to give people more than they would think to ask for. For example, at a beach house I could do white slipcovers and sisal, and sometimes that's just right. But the idea that's going to make the house hold their interest and even their affection may be more complex than a sofa covered in white denim. What is the combination of elements that's really going to make it work?

Decorators like David Hicks, who was absolutely brilliant, have written books that are filled with diagrams about which colors go together, pronouncements like, "If you use brown and blue, you can't have red, too." Somebody once said to me, "There's no such thing as a bad color, fabric, or wallpaper, just bad applications." That's more my attitude. For every rule that exists, I'm sure there's a beautiful room that breaks it. The reality is that there are no rules.

But I do think there are guidelines, things that work and make people feel comfortable. There's a terrific book, *The Decorator* by Florence de Dampierre, in which practically every decorator declares he doesn't like orange. So, of course, I decided to paint a room orange, the color of an Hermès box. It was incredible to look down the hall and see this glow, like a James Turrell light effect. But I must admit it was super-uncomfortable to be in. So I'm probably not going to advise someone to choose orange. Maybe pumpkin or pale melon in an entrance hall or a gallery, but not in a bedroom. Orange is tricky, but there are certain colors that are easy to live with. Green is one. It's very soothing, it always works, and it looks beautiful with any other shade. I remember my client Dustin Hoffman telling me that every color I ever picked for his house was green.

There is a point at which the design process becomes a bit like magic. Fusing all the ideas together into a coherent whole involves a little alchemy and a little shamanism. There are certain inexplicable gravitational pulls that I can't resist. Some decisions I make are beyond me. They're almost unconscious—I don't know exactly why I made it, yet there it is. The most extraordinary thing about being a designer is that you get to constantly immerse yourself in other lives, in other styles and cultures, and create something you've never seen before.

One of the things that gives me the most pleasure—yet it's also really torture—is to make it different every time, harder, more challenging. If a house works, it becomes greater than the sum of its parts. It takes on a life of its own. You forget how hard it was to do the foundation when you see roses climbing over the brick. The problems of actually building it evaporate, like the stages of a rocket falling away at lift-off. For me, designing a new house is about moving forward. And living in something you've created doubles the excitement.

My collection of nineteenth-century moon flasks is gathered together on an eighteenth-century English console—you get much more impact that way, rather than scattering them around the room. As you can see, I like my flowers in single-color bouquets arranged loosely, as though you just picked them in the garden and brought them in. The giltwood mirror is George III.

My House

THE VISION

I first saw this house in an ad in the *Los Angeles Times*. The photo was taken from the edge of the garden, and showed a pool with a lot of land. I wanted a house with grounds, which I'd never had before. So I went to look at it.

It was a not-very-good house by a very good architect, James Dolena, who did some very nice Hollywood Regency houses. But this was a mediocre 1950s ranch, built for a member of the Doheny family. It had everything you would want in a house, except it was all in the wrong place. It had a pool, but it was too close to the house. It had a garden, but the only room that opened to it was the master bedroom, which made no sense. You had absolutely no idea of the land when you walked in the front door. But it was an incredible piece of property, with huge eucalyptus trees. Completely overgrown, like a secret garden. And there was something else I liked. You know how there is always one element you fixate on? For me, it was the motorized gates. I thought, "Wow, to live in a house with motorized gates." So I bought it.

I knew it had privacy and quiet and I could create my own kind of world here. I just didn't quite realize the house was going to have to be torn down in the process.

Back to the beginning. I bought the house and lived in it for a year, which I highly recommend to anyone before starting a renovation. You learn how the light falls. You uncover the secrets. One night, I had the bedroom doors open to the garden and a bobcat walked in (and out again, thank goodness). Of course, the danger is that you can become complacent and sort of get used to the shortcomings. You start not to see them. But this house had so many flaws.

I asked New York architect Oscar Shamamian to work with me on the plans, and I moved out and lived in a couple of rented houses while we tore mine apart and started rebuilding. I always wonder, "Do I have enough energy or creativity saved up to use on myself?" But that's never the problem. The reason this house took so long for me to finish—almost four years—was because I was busy doing other people's projects. I was not going to put a client's house on the back burner to focus on my own. I moved forward very slowly, very methodically, and built the biggest house I could afford (not that big) at the level of quality I wanted, which basically equaled exactly the amount of money I had in the world. I was slightly naïve in anticipating what it would take to make it into the house I wanted.

The rules of building on a hillside are so strict that every time I extended five inches beyond the old foundations, I had to sink a caisson sixty feet into bedrock. I did it in six places, but fundamentally I kept to the original footprint. I was very tempted to build above certain rooms, adding a second story. I was advised not to because of cost. In hindsight, I should have gone for it. But then I remind myself, I could have built more rooms, but I already have all the rooms I can use. I wouldn't live in them.

We did a lot of site work, which involved building giant retaining walls, to create a flat, level garden to the side of the house. The retaining wall was the single most expensive component of the entire renovation, but I had to have a flat outdoor space. The infrastructure work on the site alone was a very expensive undertaking.

I took down dozens of trees to clear the plane for a new saltwater pool and, on the view side of the house, to frame the vista. Now you can see all the way to the ocean. The house is in Bel Air, and the reason this section of Los Angeles is called Bel Air is because you catch the ocean breezes up here, which was very important before air conditioning.

Basically, I bought the land and had a vision of a house in my head. I had this desire for a kind of English country house. I was doing a lot of work in England at the time for Sir Evelyn de Rothschild and his wife Lynn, and just being in houses and hotels again in London brought back all sorts of memories. I had gone to school in England, and I've always been obsessed with every Colefax & Fowler interior and any place done by Robert Adam or William Kent. My great, great, great love is English furniture and English architecture. I was also

I love Georgian architecture for its quiet blend of dignity and elegance—qualities I wanted in my own house, designed by Oscar Shamamian of Ferguson & Shamamian. The old brick has a softness that conveys age, and Oscar added lovely period details like the rusticated brick window surround. From the outside, it looks like a two-story house but that window actually illuminates a double-height entrance hall. I think there should be a sense of ceremony as you walk up to a front door, and the classical columns and portico help create it. I added two magnolia trees in Versailles tubs and a pair of early nineteenth-century leaded urns. Sport and Jasper, my Labradoodles, wait patiently in the courtyard, paved with Santa Barbara sandstone.

living in a modern house in Los Angeles at the time, so it was probably a bit of a reaction. I've always loved English houses. They're such an appealing fusion of comfort and style. And let's face it, English country style was fundamental to the creation of an American style. And it worked both ways. You had a lot of incredibly talented Southern women—Nancy Lancaster, Nancy Astor—weighing in on the English tradition. It's really an Anglo-American style.

One building that had a profound impact on me was Worcester Lodge, done by William Kent in the 1740s at Badminton. The Lodge is an incredibly elegant gatehouse in the middle of this vast rolling countryside, and it's one of the most beautiful Neoclassical follies that I've ever seen. I remember going into the sort of dining room upstairs, with white-painted William Kent chairs and a long, battered wood table, and thinking, "How wonderful." In a folly, you're not encumbered by a lot of things that a normal house needs—like a living room, which can be the most boring room to design. Living in unusual kinds of spaces can be very liberating. Look at the famous

converted carriage house that Nancy Lancaster owned. Her rooms have a sense of magic and charm that somehow isn't diminished by function. They're theater, essentially, and theater is always intriguing.

When I visit an English country house, I'm always eager to get a close look at the carriage house, the pavilions. And then there's often a little house, the dower house, for the widowed mother—grander than a cottage but not nearly as monumental as the main residence. I like the idea of the lesser house on a great estate.

So, for my own house, I developed a kind of historical fiction. I jumped paradigms, moving from the California ranch house to the English dower house. But my house is not a slavish copy of anything I've actually seen. It's my vision of a dower house, something the great English architect Sir Edwin Lutyens might have designed, if he were born in Los Angeles in instead of London in 1869. It's built of old brick, with a slate roof and Georgian details. It looks as if it has two stories from the outside. When you come in, you realize it's actually

Opposite: The French doors in the living room open to a dining terrace, shaded by giant Brazilian pepper trees. Christine London designed the garden, which feels lush and overgrown and very private. Yet if you look over the retaining wall, you can see the city and the ocean.

Above: An eighteenth-century marble copy of a Roman bust provides a focal point amid all the trees.

just one story—but with a relatively grand feeling. Oscar and I made my living room ceiling eighteen feet high, and gave it a double vault. It's pure Lutyens, gorgeous and theatrical. He really knew how to shape space. Lutyens managed to create a whole new English style by taking the best elements of other architects and putting it together, in a way that was both modern and traditional at the same time.

I love the fact that the house is very approachable from the outside, and then you step into this amazing space with very tall ceilings. It's a surprise. I wanted classically proportioned rooms and an orderly progression of spaces. I worked very closely with Oscar, and his forte was to pull all my ideas together and make it look as if they all belonged in one house.

Even with an architect in charge, everything that could go wrong did go wrong, just as it does in everybody else's house. All the fireplaces draw badly because I live in a canyon and there are these odd air currents and it's simply not fixable. Without exception, every time I light the fireplace in the master bedroom, the smoke alarms go off and the firemen come. Even more obvious is a very, very steep driveway, which I call the luge. Definitely not ideal, but there was no other choice. At least I thought I would surface it with this new material I was obsessed with. It was a test case, and it failed. It's broken up and stained and horrible, and I'll have to redo it. And of course I don't have enough closet space, which I knew would be a problem. But I could only build within the existing confines or else I had to sink more caissons.

Construction is a process that's inherently defective, just by nature of the fact that a house represents dozens and dozens of workers, relying on dozens and dozens of fabricators. It's amazing that more stuff doesn't go wrong. But when it goes right, building a house is like the ultimate barn-raising—thrilling, and very satisfying. There's a great trust that develops when everybody's working together.

Above: A table on the terrace has a concrete top—very simple and impervious to the weather. It can seat ten for an al fresco lunch or dinner. The Nice chairs are from Janus et Cie.

Opposite: The saltwater pool is made of French limestone. Instead of pushing the steps off to the side, I tried to make them part of the design. A pair of covered urns adds a sense of romance, without getting overly flowery.

My House

THE PLAN

One of my favorite rooms in a traditional English house is the entrance hall. I like the severity, the lack of ornament, and the mood that creates. In my own entrance hall, I wanted a space that felt architecturally strong and austere, a simplified drama that was really well thought out in terms of details like the cornice and vaulting. An entrance hall should create a sense of arrival. Then I wanted each room to be an individual experience, but without the showhouse effect of too many different stories under the same roof.

We were tied to the existing footprint of the house, and what the house could handle within those limits. Then there were some basic real estate decisions: Do I do a kitchen/family room to up the resale value? Or something more tailored to myself? I decided to stay close to my vision. I didn't want to cook with guests surrounding me, so that led to a separate kitchen, a breakfast room, and a formal dining room. And then there was that mental scrapbook of things I had always wanted, like a Georgian paneled library. How much of that wish list could I have? The paneled room turned out to be the master bedroom, not the library. The furnishings didn't come before the architecture, but some rooms came already tagged with a dedicated piece or a decorating idea. Still, it was important that each room be beautiful even with nothing in it.

Like many classical houses, mine was organized around the idea of a central hall. This hall is a long, wide corridor, perpendicular to the entrance hall, with the kitchen at one end and the sunroom at the other. It gives the house a strong axis and a sense of procession. It also bypasses the master bedroom, which solved the problem of how to divide the public from the private rooms in a house on a single floor. In the original plan, the only way to the garden was through the master bedroom. Now that space has become a two-story-high sunroom, that opens to the garden. It's a solution that's much more gracious and logical. The public rooms open not into each other but off this hall, which allows me to have Chinese wallpaper in the dining room and something totally different next door. It's the corridor that makes the individuality possible. It gives the spaces breathing room. It calms you, cleansing the palate as you move from one room to another. Oscar teasingly calls the house the ceiling museum, because every room has a different ceiling and its own distinctive architectural style. I admit this house does have a lot of movies in it, almost a film festival, which is something I wouldn't necessarily try for a client. But it works for me.

THE ENTRANCE HALL

I love walking into an English house and seeing a fireplace in the entrance hall. It sets that manor-house tone and makes the room feel so much warmer. My entrance hall is beautifully proportioned and is two stories high, which instantly ups the stature of the house. Oscar designed an elegant domed ceiling. Then I started playing around with colors and finishes. In John Fowler's English houses, the rooms were often a delicious pinky melon to create a sense of warmth. But the light in California is already so apricoty that the walls had to be paler. We mixed a little terra cotta dust into the Venetian plaster to give it a blush. The dome of the ceiling is limewashed, so it looks very matte. The trim color is a pale cream. In New York, you could go with a stronger color because the light flattens it. But here, light intensifies color so it has to be very subtle. There's just a little jump between the colors on the upper and lower levels, which accentuates the lines and curves of the architecture.

In a way, this is my favorite room. The proportions are perfect. It's a real break from the lush landscape

I wanted a fireplace in the entrance hall because it instantly makes me feel as if I'm in Oxfordshire. Everything from the limestone floor to the limewashed ceiling is done in various shades of white—very simple and severe. Creamy white paint—Farrow & Ball's White Tie 2002—picks out the fine lines of the columned cornice and the pediments over the doors. I kept the furnishings deliberately spare—just two benches, an Egyptian Revival chair—so people would focus on the strong bones of the room. The objects on the mantel are very early Bactrian ritual vessels made of alabaster.

outside. This is a dramatic, manmade space, and out there is nature. Inside, it's all about control. The architecture is classical. The palette is monochromatic. There are ten or twelve different textures in the room—Venetian plaster, the Turkish travertine floor, a woven straw rug—but only one color. Even the painting above the fireplace, by Beatrice Caracciolo, is white, with a stone-like texture. I like the strong, masculine lines of the Egyptian Revival–style chair. The candles in the large hurricane lights are lit at night. There are no curtains at the windows. Everything is very simple, in shades of white. I love all these pale, pale neutrals. Manuel Canovas, one of the great colorists, collects jars of sand from beaches all over the world. There's something poetic about that. What I like about this space is that there are all these different colors, but no real color.

THE LIVING ROOM

I wanted a big, classically proportioned drawing room and Oscar and I designed it specifically to accommodate a fifteen-foot-long Gillows bookcase, made in mahogany after a design by Robert Adam. I bought it years ago, and at various times it has been in my office and in storage. Finally, I would get to live with it. It's opposite a lusty painting by Joan Mitchell, which I purposely didn't hang over the fireplace. I want people to discover it.

There's a major seating group around the fireplace, and another anchored by a second sofa against a wall. Sometimes I think I should have done something more eccentric and looser. Albert Hadley is great at these floating furniture plans, but that wasn't this house, which is more classical. Besides, people like to gather around a fireplace

---

Above: One entire wall of the living room is taken up by the massive fifteen-foot-long Gillows bookcase. Robert and Richard Gillow were a father-and-son team who ran a thriving furniture business in Lancaster and London, England, during the eighteenth century. The beautifully carved Georgian armchair is covered in museum-red Fortuny fabric.

Opposite: The furniture grouped around an antique Japanese table includes a sofa upholstered in Bentley Rose hemp—a fabric I designed for my Jasper collection—a nineteenth-century Irish armchair covered in Chelsea Editions' blue-and-white Thistle, and a nineteenth-century painted library chair. Over the fireplace, I hung a painting by Christine Taber, which I like because you can't quite make it out. It has the vaporous quality of a mirror. The carpet is an antique Tabriz from Mansour.

in one big conversational cluster on comfortable sofas and generous club chairs, with a low coffee table that can serve as a plateau for books and drinks and hors d'oeuvres. I'm not sure anything else would feel as inviting.

I always specify different styles of seating. If it's all the same overstuffed chairs, the room begins to feel like a lobby. Besides, sometimes you want to sink into a sofa and other times you want to sit up straight. The fabrics here don't match, but they don't disagree—the grouping in front of the fireplace alone has half a dozen different patterns on the chairs, not to mention the antique Tabriz carpet. I love antique fabrics, with that mellow patina, and then I always throw in something a little unexpected, like the turquoise blue checked chair. Otherwise it would be too flat, too all-in-one-tone. The tiger-striped pillows also throw it off. Then the abstract painting I hung over the fireplace pushes the room into another dimension.

Finishes are a subtext in the story of any house, and here I used them to deepen the Englishness. The floors are reclaimed brown oak. The boards are wide, varied in size, and they're imperfect. I didn't use stain on the oak. They're just scrubbed and waxed. No urethane. Everybody always tries to talk me out of it, but I just think this look is so much more beautiful. Putting anything else on them never gives you the same effect. The floors require maintenance, but I think it's worth it. I also had all the hardware plated with silver. I'd have to think twice before asking a client to commit to that kind of upkeep, but the look of old silver gives the house a sense of authenticity and age. All the doors are paneled, and made of solid mahogany. There's hardly any paint in the house. It's all Venetian plaster and limewashed ceilings, which gives the surfaces more depth and substance. As for my color palette, I like odd colors—olive and putty—colors with shadows in them, colors from another era. I didn't use downlights, which would be too harsh. I prefer pools of lamplight, which is much more atmospheric.

The best houses, or rooms for that matter, are a little unpredictable. They have a life of their own. Objects come in and out. The character evolves. You don't want to over-process and direct. You want to let the house unfold.

Opposite: A second sofa against the wall anchors another seating area in the living room. Clearly, I don't believe that pillows should politely match. Instead, I use them to layer on more pattern and texture. The painting over the sofa is by Joan Mitchell.

Above: Here, I was playing with the idea of circles and sheen. The silver pieces are African, found in Seattle at Honeychurch Antiques. The painting is embedded with more circles in mother-of-pearl. I don't over-study these tablescapes. I just put things together until they look interesting.

THE LIBRARY

I wanted a cozy paneled library, but I didn't want the typical dark wood, so I had the paneling painted olive green (see a more complete view of the library on page 44). It has warmth but it's a bit severe, more like the seventeenth- and eighteenth-century rooms at Ham House and Colonial Williamsburg that I love. What was perceived as grand then is actually fairly simple—a lot of paint and a lot of oak. Very classic. Then I found this wonderful hand-blocked linen by Clarence House in blues and greens and used it for the curtains. I'm a sucker for blue and green together. I think it's a very soothing combination.

The English Regency sofa was already covered in that bright yellow French linen when I bought it, and I kept it. Behind it is an antique painted-leather screen, made by the Dutch in imitation of the Chinese. You see a lot of painted leather in the seventeenth and eighteenth centuries, and this is a remarkable piece. Great scale, and beautifully drawn. Very architectural. It adds another layer of history to the room. The coffee table is a nineteenth-century Chinese table, cut down to work in front of the sofa, with an unusual two-tiered effect. The seventeenth-century Persian rug is really worn and really, really beautiful. I love that ravaged quality.

The tall mahogany Charles X chair was something I coveted ever since I saw it in a New York antiques shop many years ago. It went through another owner or two before I was finally able to buy it. This whole room is layered with objects that I love—blue-and-white porcelain, old French maps, a marble obelisk—all calculated to transport you to another place and time. I had the mantel made in honed gray marble, copying an early eighteenth-century chimneypiece. The eighteenth-century English landscape that hangs above it hides a flat-screen TV. A lot of my books are here, and my computer. This library is the smallest room in the house, but it's probably the most used.

The dark painted-leather screen sets off the bright yellow English Regency sofa, draped with an old Indonesian quilt that I bought because I loved the pattern. Then I threw in even more pattern with the pillows, covered in a Turkish ikat and an Indian cotton. The tea table is Georgian English. The hurricane lamp is from John Rosselli.

THE DINING ROOM

The big question in the dining room was whether or not we should open it to the kitchen, given the fact that it's a narrow space and we couldn't make it any larger. But I really did want an actual dining room, so we kept it intact. Now, all I had to do was make it magical. I knew I was going to use hand-painted chinoiserie wallpaper from de Gournay, because I love it and it adds such depth to a room. When you're looking through flowering branches to brightly painted birds, you get a sense of a vista beyond the four walls. It plays with your whole sense of perception.

I hung a George II giltwood overmantel mirror on one wall and a large-scale photograph—a view of Florence by Massimo Vitale—on the other. It reads as a modern reinterpretation of an Old Master painting and keeps the room from becoming too ponderous. I bought the chandelier in Florence with the proviso that they take off all the pink glass flowers. I put candles in it and use it all the time. The sconces hold candles as well. I think there is nothing more romantic than dining by candlelight. The only electric light in the room comes from a pair of lamps by the mirror.

The table is an English Regency piece made out of particularly splendid mahogany. "Good timbers," as they say in the trade. It's surrounded by the Tyler chairs from my Jasper collection, upholstered in a beautiful silk velvet. It's just the sort of thing I love—a petroleum blue-green, peacock-feather kind of color. I like the way it plays off all the neutrals—the paper-bag color in the wallpaper, the cream curtains. It's a fabric that's bright and pretty during the day. Then at night, it turns dark and inky and becomes more dramatic and mysterious.

Opposite: In the dining room, the delicate custom-made Earlham wallpaper by de Gournay sets a dream-like mood. The English Regency mahogany table is one of the most beautiful I've ever seen, because of the quality of the wood. Whenever I see one of those Chinese monochrome porcelain vases, I pull out my checkbook. I love those burnt-red, peach-dust, and green-tea glazes.

Above: A Chinese Louhan figure, meant to guard Buddha and made of bronze, stands next to a French rock-crystal lamp on the sideboard.

THE KITCHEN

In movies like *Gosford Park*, I'm always looking at all the back-of-the-house stuff, the staff rooms. I wanted to play up the idea that this was a great old service kitchen—masculine English, not pretty English. It's smaller than I would have liked—I was restricted by the size of the old floor plan—but it's very functional. Everything is within reach. The range is a BlueStar with a broiler and a salamander—I really wanted that. It deserves a serious cook, which I am not. Then Oscar Shamamian and Joseph Singer designed the hood, with an antique pewter finish. Very Jules Verne meets the Industrial Revolution.

The countertops are made of Lagos Azul limestone. Citrus stains them. Every once in a while I'll have them professionally cleaned, but I like the fact that they're not static. It's funny. Everybody gravitates to old tables and old stone, but when it comes to their own house, they want something pristine. Not me. I try to walk the walk. If I have counters that stain and floors that need to be waxed, then I can say with great confidence, "Hey, don't be afraid. It does require some extra effort, but it's worth

it." Every piece of hardware, including the faucet and the knobs, is sterling-plated, which looks so much softer and beautiful to me than regular nickel. It's a finish that shifts with the light and looks more alive. The backsplash is made of handmade Moroccan tiles, with a beautiful, milky glaze. Each is a different color of white. Again, what's pretty is that it has so much variety from piece to piece. I tinted the grout a soft gray to suggest age.

It's actually a galley kitchen, quite compact, but no one even notices that because of the Lutyens barrel-vault ceiling. It gives a sense of ceremony to a narrow space. The kitchen feels much bigger than it is because of the ceiling height and the fact that it's laid out as a sequence of rooms—laundry, pantry, kitchen—culminating in the breakfast room, like the light at the end of a tunnel. The real trick is the enfilade, because it lets me borrow space, in a way. The architecture sets up the vista, and your eye automatically goes to the farthest point. The glass-fronted refrigerator and glass-fronted cabinets also help, because they give you a sense that there's more depth. With solid-door cabinets and a solid refrigerator, you would have felt much more closed in.

Opposite: This kitchen, with a barrel-vaulted ceiling and old-fashioned cabinetry, feels as if it should come with a butler. Even the stainless steel appliances have that professional look. The hanging lights are from Ann-Morris Antiques. The floor is reclaimed fumed brown oak from Baba, a company in North Carolina that sells fine antique floors. The kitchen opens to the breakfast room, just beyond.

Above: In the other direction, the kitchen opens to the pantry and the laundry room. I love my BlueStar RNB Heritage Classic range, with six burners, two extra-large ovens, a professional-style raised griddle, and an infrared broiler—but let's just say I'm not the one who usually cooks on it.

THE BREAKFAST ROOM

It may be unfashionable these days to define rooms instead of leaving it all one giant unformed space, but I think humans like pleasing geometries and regular shapes. The breakfast room is an octagon, just because I think it's pretty. There are five pairs of French doors, and we leave them open all the time—a standard part of the deal in California. The dogs run in and out. It's like a little temple in the garden. I have the pleasant sense of eating outside, while still being shielded from the direct sunlight. With the curtains drawn at night, you get a lovely tented effect. The pattern is based on an antique Moghul panel I found and became obsessed with. So I

had it copied, in hemp, for my Jasper collection.

Four George III mahogany chairs surround a William IV rosewood pedestal table. The mahogany Lazy Susan on top dates from the Georgian era. I bought an eighteenth-century English corner cupboard at auction because I loved the pale taupe wood and then had the other made to match. The wallpaper is my own Irina Check for Cowtan & Tout. It just finishes off the space. I'm obsessive about not having walls that are flat. I want something a little more reactive. That's why the domed ceiling is painted in limewash paint, which has this wonderful chalky quality. It always dries a little unevenly, which makes it even more beautiful to my eye. You can see the brushstrokes. You can see the quiver of light.

Above: One of the corner cupboards in the breakfast room is an eighteenth-century original and the other is a copy, but I'm not telling which is which.

Opposite: You can open all five French doors to the garden, or draw the curtains and feel as if you're dining in a tent. The fabric is Moghul Panel hemp, in burgundy, designed for my Jasper collection. The William IV rosewood table seats four, in George III mahogany chairs. Notice how the octagonal shape of the room is echoed in the octagonal pattern of the boards on the floor.

THE GUEST ROOM

I wanted something bold and overwhelming to give the space a sense of drama and found it in a painting by a student of Peter Paul Rubens. It brings a lot of movement and color into the room and somehow revalues the whole space. A big painting in a small room fools you into thinking the room is larger. The whole question of scale is one of the most fascinating subjects in design. I don't quite know how to predict what is going to be right, but I sure can tell when it's wrong. People say you shouldn't put big pieces of furniture in a small room or small pieces in a big room, but in fact it can be very interesting. If everything is on exactly the same scale, a room can look rather dull. I look at each room as a composition and make sure it has a rhythm. The skyline of furniture should go up and down.

I put a nice big chair right in front of the painting, which also shocks a few people. But if a room is completely geared to a painting, it turns into an art gallery. And then you get that drive-in movie effect that I see in so many beach houses, where every piece of furniture faces the view. That's crazy. Classically, a painting was meant to fit within the context of an interior, but somehow art has taken on such an exalted position that it trumps all the other furnishings. I think the chair brings the painting down to human scale and makes the room feel grounded and comfortable.

Oscar designed an interesting ceiling for each room in the house. The tray ceiling here has the effect of making the room seem taller. The ceiling seems to go on and on forever, since it gets a head start by

Left: There's really no need for much else when you have a floor-to-ceiling painting by a student of Peter Paul Rubens, but why stop there? I flanked it with sconces and more paintings. The Naples chandelier was designed for my Jasper collection.

Above: I like to make up a bed with a variety of linens. The red-and-white embroidered sheets and shams are Moroccan and the pillow in front is covered in an African textile. The wallpaper is my Irina Check for Cowtan & Tout.

Opposite: This bed, in another guest room, has been with me for years. It's my version of a bed that was owned by Balthus, the painter. I liked it so much I had it copied. At one point, I gilded the top. It's made of steel and hung with unbleached hemp curtains. The throw pillow is covered in antique chintz.

Above: An Italian sunburst ecclesiastical piece hangs over a nineteenth-century English chair, upholstered in a Bennison chintz. The walls are covered in an embroidered fabric I designed for Cowtan & Tout, based on a Portuguese textile.

starting three-quarters of the way up the wall. A silk-and-linen check I designed for Cowtan & Tout fills in the lower part. I had it paper-backed so it could be glued on flat. I never upholster a wall. I find the puffiness it creates a little claustrophobic.

There are a lot of rather eccentric things in the room—a Spanish painted bed, paintings of Egypt, paintings of India—and the fabric holds all the disparate parts together. It wraps the room like you'd wrap a package, and makes it feel cozy and intimate, more European. There might be bigger guest rooms, but nothing could be better.

THE MASTER BEDROOM

The design started with a leap of faith. I saw this picture of a stack of wood in an auction catalogue and decided to bid on it. It was panel-ing, although it was hard to tell what it looked like because there was no picture of the finished room. Yet I had this instinct that it could be amazing because everything else this person owned was beautiful. I was the highest bidder, and when it arrived we had to figure out how to put it together. There were no instructions. In fact, it took an English craftsman three months to do the jigsaw. I had assumed it was pine, but it turned out to be hemlock, probably late eighteenth-century, with a wonderful, chalky finish. We carefully matched it and made a few new pieces in order to make it work in my bedroom.

I couldn't find the perfect four-poster bed, but I found these Georgian posts and built a bed around them. Of course, it had to have a canopy. If you're going to spend a third of your life in bed, it might as well have a sense of ceremony. There's something special about a four-poster bed. It takes me back to being a kid playing in a fort, and fits in with my royalist fantasies. The hangings are made out of a fabric I designed, Indian Flower hemp. It's unusual, in that it's a masculine floral. The curtains are a dry, very matte silk—pale, pale blue against the chalky paneling. I don't like shiny silks. This is much more subtle.

The rug is a Sultanabad, probably a little too delicate to be in a well-trafficked room. But I love the colors so much that I don't care if it disintegrates under me. I'm going to enjoy it while it lasts. Hanging over the bedside chest is a piece of Turkish velvet I bought at auction. I've rarely seen such a blue. There are stacks and stacks of books everywhere. I'm constantly reading and doing research in bed. The dogs run in and out and jump up to join me and get mud over everything, much to my dismay. But it doesn't affect the innate serenity of the room. My bedroom lives up to my credo—that a room should be beautiful, even with nothing in it.

Beds are for lounging, and I always make them super-comfortable, with plenty of pillows and a canopy. In my bedroom, the canopy bed is hung with curtains made of a fabric I designed, Indian Flower hemp, in blue. The monogrammed bed linens are by Porthault. The cushion on the floor is meant for my dogs, but you can guess where they inevitably end up. The carpet is a very old Sultanabad, with all those blues I adore.

Above: This extraordinary chair is probably Baltic or Northern European. I bought it at Therien & Co. with the thought of using it for a client but I liked it so much I kept it for myself.

Right: It was quite a job to piece together a pile of eighteenth-century hemlock paneling and make it fit this particular room, but it was definitely worth the effort. The paneling adds instant history and makes it feel like a gentleman's retreat. The sofa is upholstered in a Madeleine Castaing stripe with an Indian quilt from John Robshaw tucked over the back. I made absolutely no attempt to hide the TV. I rather like the contrast of the sleek flat-screen Sony and the gilt-and-marble table.

THE MASTER BATH

What I had in the back of my head was the kind of English Edwardian temple of bathing that you'd find at a hotel like Claridge's in London. The space was too limited for a dressing room and a master bath, so I had to combine the two, and put the tub in the center of the dressing room. I designed the tub and the fixtures myself. It feels very gentlemanly, with an ebonized tea trolley right next to it for towels and magazines. The tub is oriented toward the view. In summer, I open the French doors and feel as if I'm bathing outside.

Years ago, I bought an English table with an Egyptian alabaster top for Cindy Crawford. I really loved that piece. It was part Indiana Jones and part Merchant Ivory. I thought of it again when I was designing the steam shower. The only thing I could find that looked equally dramatic was this golden ochre-colored onyx. So I ordered it and Oscar designed this elegant flat-panel detail and had it installed. Then I had a little panic attack. It was so dramatic that I wanted to tear it out. My boyfriend, James Costos, pleaded with me, begging, "Please don't tear it out. It's the only cool, modern thing in the house." Once the big octagonal showerhead and the nickel faucets were installed, it started to look very 1930s and it all clicked in and I calmed down a bit. Now it's one of my favorite things in the house.

Opposite: In the master bath, the centerpiece is definitely the Town tub with old-fashioned fittings, all part of my collection for Kallista. Because of limited space, the bath had to double as a dressing room. I'm hoping I'll never have to press my clothes, with all the steam.

Above: When I sink down into the bath, I can look straight out the French doors to the garden. The French Neoclassical stool, made out of fruitwood, is probably early nineteenth century.

THE SUNROOM

When Oscar and I designed this house we reshuffled the deck and put the rooms in a better order. The payoff, of course, was the sunroom. I needed something that connected the house to the garden. I had this fantasy of a garden room, a glass pavilion. There's a room I have only seen in two grainy photos, a room that Renzo Mongiardino, the masterful Italian decorator, did for Lee Radziwill in Oxfordshire in England. There was a remarkable lightness to that space. It had Chinese wallpaper with birds and real birds in cages, lots of straw and wicker, and a beautiful stone-topped coffee table with a bamboo base. Horst took the photos, with Lee walking through looking very glamorous, and I thought, I want a sunroom like that.

I love that room, but mine has very little relationship to Horst's famous photograph. It's my own vision of it. For me, nothing is ever pure, which is why I particularly admire Mongiardino. What he does in an English house is a whole different thing. It changes the game. You have the warmth and prettiness of an English house, but it's sexier, with a more exotic Mediterranean spirit and a certain throwaway chic. Mongiardino's sunroom inspired mine, but if you look at the rooms, they are by no means exactly alike. They do share the idea of easy accessibility to the garden, and they're both double-height. But the organization of furniture is very different. Mongiardino makes a passage through his space, and I created more of a conversational grouping around a low table. I have a chair by Jacob, a side table by John Dickinson, and a sofa covered in a kind of Indian floral I designed for Cowtan & Tout. It's a sitting room that really feels more like an indoor courtyard, since you're sharing the space with fifteen-foot-tall palm trees. The floor is Turkish travertine, which continues out onto the terrace so you're meant to feel half-in, half-out. There's a Nancy Lorenz painting above the sofa in gold leaf and mother-of-pearl, and huge Neoclassical plaster plaques on the wall. The effect of all this is very rich and strange, and utterly personal.

The double-height sunroom with its wall of French doors gives you the sensation of being outside while you're still in the house. The furnishings are eclectic, to say the least. Look at that quirky white plaster John Dickinson table to the left of the blue chair. The coffee table is another unusual piece. I bought it in Brussels but it's probably Japanese. The black lacquer surface is scattered with bits of mother-of-pearl and trimmed in red. I've never seen another like it.

I found the carved and gilded armchair by Jacob at the Steinitz Gallery in Paris. A Tang horse stands on a Russian commode that I bought at auction in Sweden. The mirror is French Régence. One of the most interesting things about the room is something you'd never guess. Both of those doors in the corner are false. Oscar Shamamian and I added them to the room for architectural symmetry. That should tell you just how obsessive Oscar and I can be.

The Process

BEGINNINGS

I have crushes on places. Right now, it's Mallorca, where I'm designing a house. I speak my four words of Spanish with a Catalan lisp. I'm driving around in my car listening to old recordings of warbling Mallorcan folksingers. It's really a throwback to my childhood, this obsession thing. And it has become the way I work. The best part is that I'm able to have multiple crushes at the same time: Mallorca. London. Montana. Millbrook. Malibu. Anywhere I'm doing a house.

It starts like this. I immerse myself in the particular aesthetic, trying to take it all in. To really understand it, I have to take it apart, identifying the various influences, threads, elements. And then when I do the house, I put it back together again in a way that's more interesting to me. I'm trying to build a better widget.

For example, some of the historic houses in Mallorca have this particular kind of decorative painting on the walls. It almost looks like a pale, pale plaid. That

---

Above: This rendering of the Mallorca project, painted by Mark Matuszak, shows the living room. The stenciling on the walls, inspired by a decorative element I saw in an old Mallorcan finca, gives a new house a sense of tradition. Instantly, the room feels softer, more broken-in. The pattern seems to connect all these dissimilar objects and hold them together.

Opposite: Here, in a subtle way, I'm playing with shapes. There are circles in the painting, the drawing, the clock, the cameo. Then there are squares—and diamonds—in the frames, the wallpaper, and on the early nineteenth-century Russian desk. And finally, to add that one note of deep lapis lazuli blue with the lamp feels very Russian to me.

seems distinctive, iconic. I could do my own version of it in the master bedroom. Then I walked into Joan Miró's studio—he lived and worked in Mallorca for twenty years, until his death in 1983. The place is much as he left it, with paint cans still open and splotches of paint on the floor. It was great to see the work, but I was really riveted by this huge wall of stone—big, cut boulders. Can I use that? And what about his palette, those bold reds and yellows, blues and blacks?

I'm always hunting for ideas. And simply by having been decorating for so long, and looking so hard at English, French, Portuguese, Italian, Mallorcan things, I can borrow them and put them together in different ways. With each country, each culture, I just add more crayons to the box.

I'm a perpetual student, eager to absorb new information. At the beginning of my career, I cobbled together my own oddly diverse education. One summer, I worked for Gep Durenberger, the renowned antiques dealer in San Juan Capistrano. Gep is devoted and tireless. I went to Europe with him on a buying trip, and we drove all day through the English countryside, going through one

warehouse after another in search of the perfect object. He introduced me to that fraternity of people who love and chase down beautiful things—contemporary art collectors, antiques dealers, interior designers. These days, a lot of dealing is done via computer, but back then you had to physically go to the ends of the earth to track down amazing things. Diana Vreeland used to call them style points, and Gep showed me how to put a room together around these style points—and how, just by changing its context, a piece could change dramatically. He specialized in early eighteenth- and nineteenth-century countrified pieces, masculine and reductive. The spareness of his style really influenced me.

Then I enrolled at Otis, the art and design school in Los Angeles. It was a great experience, to be flung together with a lot of artists and do purely creative projects. But I realized fairly quickly that the program there, which was called interior architecture, was not really what I wanted. It was great to focus on cutting-edge design, but it didn't encompass enough history and tradition for me. Through Gep, I met Bill Blass and John Saladino and Imogen Taylor, who was then at Colefax & Fowler—people who

---

I love all these reds and oranges. To me, they work together the same way blues and greens do. The French commode in red tortoise is probably from the 1960s. The embroidered textile hanging above it is Greek. Somehow the two patterns balance each other out, against the more subtle backdrop of the fabric on the wall—a wool stripe I had woven in Scotland for my Jasper collection.

were important in the world of decorating and furniture. Under their influence, I decided I should go to England and study at the Victoria & Albert Museum, in its decorative arts program. That gave me an amazing overview, and just to be in Europe and see all those great houses was an education in itself.

The rooms I always remember best are entrance halls. In an English house, you have to reveal your hand in the entrance hall, in a subtle way, and introduce the narrative. I was fascinated by how they were organized. Some were almost propagandistic, in a way. At Blenheim, you get the story immediately. It's an amazing kind of Leni Riefenstahl creation, all about telling the world we are powerful and rich and unshakable. You're dwarfed by the soaring architecture and the monumental furniture and that elaborate brass lock, the size of a baby, on the door. It was incredibly intense.

England was the first culture in which I totally immersed myself. Which is good, because the idea of English country style is so pivotal to my work. It's the original hybrid, furnished with the spoils of all those colonies. And it's a delightful cross between English eclecticism and Southern comfort, because the style we think of as pure English is actually half the creation of two Americans—Nancy Astor and Nancy Lancaster, both from Virginia.

One of the touchstones in the history of decorative arts is Nancy Lancaster's "buttah" yellow room. She took a very grand space—John Nash's drawing studio—and made it cozy, transforming the gray light of London with all that yellow paint. There were billowing yellow silk curtains at the windows, mirrored panels around the doors, and a very eccentric collection of furniture that somehow looked completely comfortable. The room still holds together today.

Colefax & Fowler were a big influence on me because they were the first to do that provocative combination of high and low. It was a way of taking some of the formality and stiffness out of very grand rooms. They weren't afraid to be theatrical. Or irreverent, hanging a child's drawing next to a Picasso.

When I returned to the United States, I worked for John Saladino in New York and came away with a real appreciation for his talent and his personal style. His own houses are extraordinarily beautiful. He decided how he wanted to live and made it happen.

This octagonal vestibule in a guesthouse in Malibu is all about pattern and shape. Many years ago, I bought all these Greco-Roman mosaic panels at auction and stored them until I found the right place for them. Along with the antique vases, they give a new house another, more ancient storyline. The bench looks as if it could have come out of the Villa Kerylos—a re-creation of an ancient Greek villa built by a French archaeologist in the 1900s on the Cote d'Azur. And then I threw in a Chinese paper lantern, because nothing I do is ever purely one period or culture.

We're all basically trying to do the same. Designers can just visualize it easier than others. So many dealers helped hone my eye. Niall Smith, who started in Biedermeier and went on to William Morris and Irish furniture, was pivotal for me.

He and Jean-Claude Ciancimino, who now specializes in twentieth-century and Asian furniture, showed me that furniture could really be interior architecture. Ciancimino's shop in London was the source for a lot of those great wooden staircase models that Bill Blass collected. Will Fisher at Jamb in London is another exceptional dealer. In a great dealer's shop, you realize that furniture could be as powerful as sculpture. You could put one piece of furniture in an empty room—if it was the right piece of furniture—and it would hold its own in space. In Paris, I never missed Ariane Dandois and Madeleine Castaing, two visionaries who always had the most eccentric and yet surprisingly beautiful objects in their shops. Amy Perlin in New York finds the most masculine, sculptural furniture in beautiful woods. Michael Trapp in Connecticut combines ruined, weathered objects in the most extraordinary vignettes. I'll buy something from him simply because it looks so compelling, even though I have no idea where it's going to go.

A great dealer will give you that amazing edit—an inspired arrangement of furniture that makes even the most familiar object feel like a new discovery. Every year, I look forward to seeing what Philip Perrin has put together for his booth at the Maastricht art and antiques fair. Then I look across the way at an art dealer and there's a Rothko hanging on the wall, and I realize that everything Philip has in his booth wouldn't fetch as much as that one painting. Furniture is incredibly undervalued given the price of art. Most pieces I love are still affordable. I never tire of the hunt.

This vignette off a coatroom—made up of a seventeenth-century coffer, a Chinese figure, a shell, a contemporary work on paper—is about putting things together that have the same kind of vibration. They're all dark and very linear, with the contrast of the white shell and the gray stone. These are natural materials that have their own inherent color and texture. In the background is a very early English table—more dark and light—standing on another Greco-Roman mosaic.

COLLECTING

I'm fascinated with the idea that personality is something you can capture in a room. When it comes to people's houses, I'm an anthropologist—sizing up who they are from the books on their shelves and the pictures on their walls and the objects they collect.

When I started collecting, the first things I bought were definitely against the trend—vases and dishes made of bits of broken glass and beads, like a do-it-yourself version of Palissy ware. I remember being at a flea market in Michigan and buying vases with shells and rocks glued on and thinking, "This is really weird and kind of ugly." Yet at the same time I was really attracted to it. And then I started to see similar things everywhere.

It's not that I go out of my way to be ahead of the pack. I just get bored quickly. While most people are still entranced with the trend of the moment, I'm already moving on. I notice something from a period I haven't thought of in a while and suddenly see possibilities. Right now, I'm buying Liberty document fabrics and old Arts & Crafts furniture. I'm putting bright William Morris linens on Bentwood chairs, and looking at Gustav Klimt's Byzantine colors and organic forms. I never liked Chinese cloisonné before, and now I'm obsessed with its depth of color and the simplicity of the shapes. I can see it on the horizon. Sometimes these shifts appear first in fashion, in the couture shows. Or you can see it coming from the

Above: A Khmer torso and a Ghandaran face are surrounded by a collection of Chinese bartering objects, some made of ivory and some made of stone. The Chinese stone table adds more texture, all in the same natural palette of ivory and terra cotta and gray.

Opposite: In the library of my own house, the furnishings—an antique Dutch painted-leather screen, an English Regency sofa, a nineteenth-century Chinese table—represent an assortment of cultures and periods. But my particular favorite is that tall mahogany Charles X chair, which I first spotted many years ago in a New York antiques shop at a time when I couldn't afford it. But things have a way of coming round again, and when this chair reappeared in my life, I didn't let it slip away again.

A collector can never have too much wall space. In this London drawing room, paintings are even hung over the doors and become a kind of architectural element. The painting above the sofa is by Joseph Wright of Derby, an eighteenth-century English Romantic painter who was a master of chiaroscuro—the depiction of light and shade. Here his subject is a grotto in Salerno, Italy.

ground up in flea markets, where dealers have focused on something because it's overlooked and inexpensive—until the pendulum swings in the opposite direction.

I've been going to flea markets and antiques shows since way back. They taught me to be fast, to quickly scan a stall and pick out anything exceptional. I do the blink, and see if anything catches my eye. I don't like to linger. After speeding through the Modernism show in Santa Monica with a client in tow, he turned to me and said, "Thank you for that. I hadn't had my cardio today." I like to zip through and note pieces I want to go back and examine. I rarely miss anything, because I've been doing it for so long. I automatically zero in on the things that are special. You've got very little time, and the competition can be fierce.

Auctions are also time-sensitive, which heats up the atmosphere and makes it exciting. You can win or lose. It's like a roll of the dice. You can buy something but spend too much, or lose out on something you really like because your bid was too low. The discipline comes in deciding what you are willing to pay for an object, and sticking to that limit. If I lose it, so be it. There will always be something else.

And if you wait long enough, everything comes back. Years ago, I saw a Charles X chair in Juan Portela's shop on Madison Avenue. I loved it, I wanted it, I couldn't afford it. Eventually it made its way through the process and ended up back in his shop, and by the time the shop's contents were auctioned off, I could afford the chair. It's now in my library. There's no such thing as never again.

I often see a piece for sale and know I've seen it before, usually in an old auction catalogue. I study these catalogues, and make an effort to acquire old ones from important sales like Mentmore—a magnificent English country house whose contents were auctioned off in 1977, or the Wrightsman French furniture auction in 1984. I'm constantly thumbing through old catalogues, books,

---

Above: I've been watching various English nineteenth-century Aesthetic Movement pieces, like the bed and cabinet in this rendering, come up on the market. They're relatively inexpensive and very beautifully made. The cabinet shows off a collection of blue-and-white porcelain—a perennial classic that gives a sense of history to a room.

Opposite: These are two very different pieces of Italian furniture that I put together—a country Tuscan painted table and a more grand gilded chair. Then I added a Renaissance architectural fragment and a little Chinese garden stool. Once again, I'm playing with texture and shape.

and magazines. I still look at Rosamond Bernier's books on European decorating. I reread the articles Mark Hampton wrote on decorating for *House & Garden* in the 1980s.

A lot of people will tear out a favorite picture or two from a magazine and toss the rest. I never cut out anything, because I don't know when I'll go back and look through the same pages and fixate on something else. I'll see a Gae Aulenti sectional sofa from the 1970s, and maybe I didn't like it five years ago but I'm captivated by it now. Taste is an ever-evolving thing. One day something you've always dismissed suddenly looks attractive. Even the most cartoonish Memphis furniture from the 1980s now has its own kind of romance for me. I've never really liked lacquered walls, but I was just looking at a photo of the taxicab-yellow drawing room Sister Parish did for Babe Paley, and I think I want to revisit that. When I was eleven, I picked out Marimekko ladybug fabric for my bedroom. Now Marimekko is back. The idea is never to become rigid or closed to anything. I'm having a vermeil moment right now.

If I love something, I never quite leave it. I just file it away in my memory bank. I'm trying to find a Julian Schnabel broken-plates painting because I think they're so beautiful and important and we've forgotten how great they are. For one project, I'm searching for a very 1960s-modern fabric that used to be called glass curtains. I remember one particular style that even had ostrich feathers woven in, so I called up the showroom where I saw them and was told they haven't been produced for twelve years. Well, it just proves how long I can hold on to an idea. I had it in my head that one day I would use them. Maybe if I wait a little longer, they'll come back.

Chinese scholar's rocks, like the two in special mounts on the Chinese painting table, are natural formations of rock that were collected and appreciated for their particular shape or color or markings. I like to see them in relation to the Ghandaran torso. To me, the hand-carved folds of the statue's drapery feel very modern, and the rocks themselves could be contemporary sculptures.

STRATEGY

People are terrified of their own taste. They think they're going to do something wrong. So they would prefer to replicate something they have already seen instead of creating something of their own that's fluid and organic.

All the decorating books out there—French style, Moroccan style, Ukrainian style—make the problem even worse, creating the impression that there is one correct version of each style, separate and unique. But I'm not sure any of my clients really want to live in a purely Moroccan house. And no one these days could live in an English Georgian house without suppressing elements of their personality. I think houses that are too pure in style

start to feel like a museum. They're boring. You eventually tire of them. You shouldn't feel the prisoner of rooms that force you to live in a certain way.

Part of the problem with style as we know it is that people fear going beyond the familiar and changing direction. But we're all drawn to very different things. A room will be much more interesting if we allow ourselves to express them. To get to the essence of what you really want, you have to dig through a lot of layers of what you feel is expected or prestigious or impressive. You have to work to find it.

When I'm designing a room, there's a part of the process that's rational and a part that's kind of magic.

Above: In this guest bedroom in London I used Fortuny fabric on the walls, but on the wrong side. Somehow that softened the contrast of the yellow and white and made it even more textural. I love Fortuny fabric because of that hand-blocked batik quality—so much more interesting than ordinary flat fabric. You can't replicate it with anything else.

Opposite: This beach house was designed by architect Richard Meier and my work here is not about decorating. It's about staying out of the way of the architecture and picking up the voice of the house. Simple furnishings with strong shapes, in natural materials—like the oak coffee table and the hemp-covered sofa—seem to follow the same planes and echo the organic textures of the building itself. The painting is by Brice Marden.

A lot of external forces come into play. First, I try to deal with all the needs, desires, and personalities of the people who are the clients. Do they have children? Do they like color? Do they have a collection of American folk art? What are the pieces they will bring into the house? What is personal to them?

On the other side, in my head I draw up a list. What is the house that they're buying or building? What are they responding to? Is it the style—Georgian, Mediterranean, Spanish hacienda? What are the restrictions? Can the house only be a certain size? What is the context? Is it in a place that has a strong architectural identity, like Martha's Vineyard? Is it a classic apartment building on Park Avenue by Rosario Candela?

Where do the personal and the context converge? A house should have a sense of personality as well as a sense of place. Context is relatively simple. It's the givens you have to work with, the facts. But getting the personal right—channeling people's likes and dislikes, their quirks and foibles—is really an art. The personal is complex and often hard for people to explore on their own. And being personal is not only a matter of who people are but who they aspire to be. They may want to feel taller or smarter, to have more books than they could ever read. That's perfectly all right. I even think it's healthy.

A lot has been written about couples that have different tastes, and there are movies and television shows that make it comical. I've never had a problem with it. In any relationship, between any two people, there are common threads. I don't think anybody should have to give up his or her desires. Perhaps the husband likes contemporary things and the wife likes traditional. That's the cliché. But I think the two together are actually more interesting. You can meld them. But each has to be equally strong. You can't diminish one idea to make way for the other.

Everything that we love in life—fragrance, food, fashion, art—is about the contrast and tension between elements. It's the medley of flavors that makes a dish taste good. It's the juxtaposition of color and line and shape that makes an artwork resonate.

I designed this library in a house on Martha's Vineyard to feel as if you were actually on a ship. The richness is in the wood. Everything else needed to be slightly plain. A sea-captain's chest serves as a coffee table. The convex mirror over the fireplace could be mistaken for a porthole. There's a beautiful washed-out linen on the oversize club chair, which is where I would curl up and read. It's a warm, masculine room. No fuss. No frills.

The hybrid has an inner tension that gives it life. That's what makes us respond, and that's what I think houses need to have. They should be multidimensional, just like their owners. You're informed about the person and who they are by the rooms in which they live. Everyone picks up on that. You know when you go to someone's house if they are comfortable in their space and if they're surrounded by objects they love, not just objects the decorator dropped off. There's nothing worse than rooms that are completely unconnected to the people who live there. I don't know how to do that kind of work.

The contrast or tension in the hybrid is the easy part for me. I'm constantly thinking in images from all sorts of cultures. The hard part is to get the background right, to perfect the bones and the structure of the house. Only then can I pivot off into some flight of fancy or an odd twist. Before I begin, I need to find the idea, the vision, which is the sap line of the project. Then I start cross-pollinating by adding more and more references. And the reality is, the hybrid concept—with its indefinable, unpredictable mix of elements—is what allows me to be able to do two or three or six houses for the same people and have each of them be distinctive and different. The deck is reshuffled. There are constants, but the outcome always changes.

It's kind of like the way a good chef cooks. Some people see a recipe for baked apples in the *New York Times* and go to the store and buy every single ingredient and put it together exactly the way the recipe says. So, not surprisingly, you have the same result. It's a formula. Not tailored or personalized. But a chef may start off with a recipe for baked apples and instead decide, I'm going to find beautiful organic pears. Instead of vanilla, I'm going to add rum. It's about personalizing and putting your own stamp on things.

Take something like animal prints. By now we've seen everything in the world from leopard to zebra. The saturation of that idea is so complete that I'd have a hard time doing an on-the-nose version. It's going to have to come out in some other way than the typical leopard carpets. Maybe I would use cowhide for a library floor. Sometimes I give a twist to something that's a little tired by changing its context. I might take a pair of Victorian curtains and make them into top cushions for a linen sofa.

Suddenly the sofa creates a whole different impression. I'm sampling, just like a rapper.

Boredom for me is a great motivator. I need to keep challenging myself, to make it harder each time in order to keep on my game. I don't like doing the same thing over and over. Instead, I'm constantly trying to find new materials, new sources. The search is risky and time-consuming, but it keeps me fresh. I'll say to my staff, "Let's try this new upholsterer. What about this man who makes boiserie in Paris? But instead of traditional boiserie, let's do it sort of Ruhlmann-esque, maybe palmwood paneling combined with a twentieth-century material like parchment or leather. Could be very rich." Sometimes I start with the idea of linen curtains and then go through every possible alternative until I come back full circle to linen curtains, because sometimes linen curtains are the best idea. But I'm always trying to figure out a more interesting way of doing things. I want to open it up to everything.

For months, I've been obsessing about this Park Avenue apartment. It's a really exceptional space—wrap-around terraces with views of the city and Central Park, incredible Rosario Candela architecture that has never been touched. The vision is that this is a European villa in New York. I'm doing eighteenth-century parquet de Versailles floors and boiserie doors. But what should I put on the drawing room walls? I don't think it's paint. Is it Chinese wallpaper? Silk? An odd stripe? I'm waiting for an idea to rise to the surface. I don't want to rush it. Over time, I've learned to respect my process. What I put on these walls will really define the space and give it another dimension. I don't want to pick too soon, before the room takes shape. It should be a little bit eccentric, to put a spin on the seriousness and turn the apartment in a different direction. If I could get enough antique Japanese fabric, I just might use that. It's hard to figure out what will give me the right effect. Do I have to go to India to find it? I could do a fancy damask, but that would be cheating. Too predictable. It's not that I'm indecisive or in a turmoil. The idea is just gestating. For every opportunity, there are a hundred choices that will be discarded. I may end up doing that drawing room wall last. What would be perfect? Donghia? Fortuny? I'm waiting to see an ikat I had specially woven in Thailand. This is the kind of thing that keeps me up at night.

In this library, I wanted to add a little exoticism to the classic English mix so I had another hand-woven ikat custom-made for me in Thailand and put it on the walls between the paneling. Antique Hispano-Moroccan tiles add another shape, another pattern. They're an unexpected touch on an eighteenth-century gilded table that would have looked more staid and serious without them.

DISSONANCE

At a dinner party the other night, a woman asked me what my childhood room was like. She said, "It must have been beautiful." And I said, "That wasn't my thing." History was my thing. I would go off on these historical binges. When I was eleven, I read *Shogun* and got this Japanese thing in my head. I wanted to eat only Japanese food, read only books about Japan. Then I'd have a Russian phase and read all about the Russian Revolution and eat blinis and sour cream. I would become completely immersed in another country, another time. I channeled

Russia. I channeled Japan. Now I'm doing a big house in Mallorca, and I've immersed myself in the culture, the history, and the food of Mallorca.

And the interesting thing is, I never end up exactly where I thought I would. I see something else or something will happen and I sort of change direction. I may start off thinking, "I want this room to be Spanish," and then I'll find a Dutch cupboard I like and put it in. Many times I'll buy something that seems unrelated, but it turns out that there's a connection. "Oh, this table is beautiful. I love it. What is

Above: This is the guest bedroom in the penthouse suite at the Lowell in Manhattan, but it has none of that generic hotel quality. Instead, the furnishings are eclectic and personal. The Dutch leather screen, unexpectedly placed behind two Louis XVI–style painted beds, becomes a virtual headboard and contrasts neatly with the smooth, ochre-yellow leather upholstering the beds. Then I threw in an African pillow—another texture and pattern.

Opposite: This composition is about taking historic objects and putting them together in a modern way, which is more about shape than content. The Chinese candlesticks and the inlaid chest were chosen for the strength of their geometries, and then I set a Japanese rafter-tail on the floor, simply because I liked its sculptural quality. The Chinese table echoes the proportions of the seventeenth-century painting of Malta.

it?" "It's Mexican." But somehow it works in the room, and later I find out it was made by Spanish craftsmen. Nothing in life is pure. No history, no culture, is pure.

And how could I, born and raised in Newport Beach, California, deliver a purely Spanish interior anyway? Why try? Why not, in fact, go the other way and multiply the references? That's when it gets interesting. Claridge's, one of my favorite hotels in London, may be quintessentially English, but it's not purely Georgian or Victorian. It's more like Georgian architecture seen through an Art Deco eye. It's a hybrid.

The hybrid exists everywhere, and I guess you could call that my guiding principle. I don't love the word itself—sounds a bit clinical. But it's fundamental to my work, which is about weaving together all sorts of images to make a house that will wear well. I believe that there's strength in the hybrid. Cross-pollination creates stronger plants, and it's the strongest kind of idea. Think of the American heiress Barbara Hutton building a Japanese house in Cuernavaca, Mexico, if you can wrap your mind around that.

The strength of the hybrid comes from the tension between elements. Two ideas together make each other stronger. It's like Ghandaran sculpture, which combines the iconography of Buddhism with Greek influences. Or British Colonial furniture made in imitation of English furniture, or Italian furniture made when Napoleon controlled Northern Italy. All of these are infinitely more interesting than the straight idea.

Chocolate flavored with mint or with orange is more tempting than plain old chocolate. I respond to the subtlety, the complexity of the flavors. Anything that makes the brain wheels turn a little faster is good, as far as I'm concerned. The concept of the hybrid interior allows me to combine things in a much more freewheeling, eccentric way, and a design with eccentricity is inherently easier to live with. It's less tight, less perfect, less constrained. Hybrid rooms are not unlike people with a diverse, multicultural background. Those are the people and the ideas and the rooms I've always been drawn to. Think of a piece of music. It's those unexpected notes, the dissonance—not the predictable chords—that makes it memorable.

If you visit Lord Leighton's house in London, you walk into this amazing entrance hall lined with Islamic and Hispano-Moroccan tile. The architecture is still very nineteenth-century English, but it's totally unexpected to virtually re-create a tile mosque in a Victorian entrance hall. That's the sort of thing I find incredibly inspiring.

A hybrid makes the most successful kind of house. When clients of mine bought a beautiful property in Santa Barbara, at first there was talk of doing a straight Italian house. Then I had one of those "blink" moments (in the words of Malcolm Gladwell), one of those moments when you suddenly see instinctively what you should do. I said, "You know, everybody is building an Italian house. Why not do something different? What about Portuguese?" Actually, it wasn't a complete left turn.

This project in the Hamptons takes the idea of English country and pushes it in a new, fresh direction, toward the English Aesthetic Movement and Orientalism. There's a Chinese wallpaper on the walls and a James McNeil Whistler portrait over the fireplace. The table behind the sofa could have been designed by the Victorian architect E. W. Godwin. It's a pretty room, with a slightly bohemian feel. Only an artist would appreciate the interesting lines of the caned chair and put it right in the center of the living room. The rendering was done by Mark Matuszak.

The landscape, the climate of Santa Barbara and Portugal are similar—in fact, I later found out that both were importing eucalyptus trees from Australia at about the same time. There are many similarities and crossovers.

So I went to Portugal to visit historic houses and buy furniture and look for architectural elements. And I realized that Portuguese style is by its very nature hybrid. Based on the country's economic dominance through the centuries—Portugal ruled the seas, with an empire that stretched from India to Africa to Brazil to Macau—it influenced many places and was influenced in return. The woods alone in the furniture can be traced to all these exotic locales. There are French, Indian, Chinese, and South American aspects to Portuguese design.

I took advantage of it all. In the Santa Barbara house, I covered the living room walls with blue-and-white tiles, halfway up—like an ornamental wainscot—a detail you'd see in a traditional Portuguese house. The tiles bring the summer heat down an instant twenty degrees. I went to Urban Outfitters and bought two hundred Indian bedspreads and chopped them up and put them on the walls and ceiling and used them as curtains and upholstery in the poolhouse. I filled the rooms with French, Indian, Italian, and Moorish furniture. Tile walls, pagoda roofs, South American woods. All the cultures were commenting on one another—much more interesting than just putting red against yellow.

The other day, I was thumbing through a book and came across pictures of a townhouse designed by Ward Bennett for Jane Wenner. In one room, Bennett might mix Indian furniture and a Picasso and modern tables of his own design. Looking at all those different things, you start to see this amazing shuffle. It's like the way a musician will borrow a piece of music. He'll sample a few bars and incorporate it into his own song.

In the same way, the hybrid allows me to create my own riffs, to be flexible and elastic without getting stuck on a formula. You can do a room of eighteenth-century furniture and then find an incredible Navajo rug and hang it on the wall for a whole new feeling. A master decorator like Albert Hadley will often add one unexpected element that completely changes the direction of a room. I try to do a room so that if the client decides to replace his Old Master drawings with contemporary photography, it will still look fine. All those things can be interchangeable. In a hybrid house, adding a new element will not sink the design. It's just another note.

For a house in Santa Barbara, I had eighteenth-century Portuguese tile copied and ran it halfway up the walls, in traditional Portuguese style. The Agra rug has a similar sort of pattern. Then there's an Italian mirror, Chinese export bowls. A house like this—a Portuguese finca in Southern California—is a hybrid. I like to shuffle the deck and come up with unexpected combinations. The furniture, except for the slipper chair in red antique damask, is shrouded in white, which feels clean, cool, and relaxed.

Picasso and Portraiture
Representation and Transformation

VERSAILLES

SPARK

It's always a challenge to communicate verbally what I see internally. I'm usually better off trying to do it visually. For every project in the office, we put together a basket of things that inspired the design. Inside, you might find a piece of broken tile, an antique textile, a chunk of driftwood. I'm trying to crystallize an idea, to show the client what set the whole thing off.

For one New York apartment, it was a postcard of the dining room of Napoleon and Josephine's Malmaison, with its striking black-and-white tile floor and pale green and melon-colored walls. I probably bought it when I was seventeen and visiting Paris, that's how long I've been carrying it around. Beside it is a Wedgwood plate that I like for its shadowy, matte color and a scrap of beautifully textured raw silk.

Sometimes I think I should start with the rug, like other decorators, but that would be far too easy. I approach the whole process in a different way. What is the vision? Think of the room as a pool of water. What's your experience when you dive in?

This is not necessarily something I would discuss with every client. It could sound a little over the top.

Above: I was after a different kind of urban glamour for the penthouse suite at the Lowell hotel in Manhattan. To make the wallpaper, I had de Gournay copy seventeenth-century Japanese screens onto gold tea paper, for a quiet shimmer. The campaign bed is made of steel. The curtains are raw silk. The materials are simple, yet luxurious. I didn't want it to look like a hotel. I wanted it to feel like a house.

Opposite: For the dining room of the suite, I had a Serge Roche mirrored table copied. There's something magical about mirror—it dematerializes space and objects—and antiqued mirror has an even softer quality. With the mirrored table and the greenhouse glass, the room is all about light and air.

But it is part of my internal process. I'm inventing a mythology for each room. It has to tell a story. Only then will it have personality. Sometimes I build up the idea very, very big, and then I take it way down. It has to suit the client, above all, and make him feel comfortable. In the office, we do notebooks with pictures of all the major furniture and samples of fabric. We do floor plans, furniture plans, and three-dimensional renderings. We want the client to have a clear picture of what he's getting every step of the way.

I like to think I can do anything, but I have to qualify that. I can do anything I think is right, which comes back to my own taste. I tend to be very orderly about space. I'm most comfortable sitting in a sofa that has its back against the wall. For me, it's almost primal. I like to feel safe and enveloped. Frankly, I never sleep as well as I did when I was a child, curled up in my twin bed against a wall. Now, when I go into a chic baby store and see a round crib in the center of the room, my reaction is, "Who are you kidding?" It makes me nervous.

So when I'm designing a living room I naturally want to put a sofa against a wall and two chairs opposite it. Some designers might find that boring. The reality is, it's soothing. Most people prefer it that way. But sometimes I think I ought to break out of that habit. I remember a room Albert Hadley did years ago with dark, dark floors, just one chintz and no rug. The furniture kind of floated in space. I don't know if I could live like that. I'm all about layering and structure. The floor is connected to the rug and the rug is connected to the sofa—like the leg bone connected to the hip bone. I like things to be tethered in space.

For me, a room just feels better if it's anchored by a carpet, something that holds it together. That's a basic principle, and there's no point in fooling around with certain things that just work. I know what those basics are, but then there are an infinite number of ways to get there. That's where I'll put my energy, into figuring out which way I'll take this time.

If a client asks me to do a beach house, I could just back up a truck and unload all this blue-and-white furniture. That would be the classic beach

Left: Here, I've adopted the English idea of furnishing a bathroom as if it were a room. There's a chair and a dressing table, lit by a lamp. An English mirror hangs over a mahogany serving piece outfitted with a sink. A collection of early American silhouettes is grouped on the wall over the tub. This is a room where you might want to linger, not merely pass through. The rendering is by Mark Matusak.

Pages 67–68: I imagined a young couple staying in the Lowell's penthouse suite, and wanted to convey a sense of richness without being heavy or pretentious. There's a comfortable sofa, a pair of chairs from my Jasper collection—painted and gessoed and covered in silk velvet. Alabaster lamps, a coffee table covered in parchment, and an antique Tabriz add to the cool, reductive play of color and texture.

house, with white slipcovered sofas in the living room—sofas you can get in any town in America. We've all seen it a hundred times. But before you dismiss it, there is that wonderful feeling of sinking into a white slipcovered sofa, especially at the beach, and that's very hard to argue with. It's like a pair of Levi's 501 jeans. There's simply nothing better, and sometimes simple is best.

So I'll do the best possible version of a white slipcovered sofa. It will be the most beautifully made, the most comfortable, with the most interesting texture to the fabric. I'll take the idea and enrich it, but subtly. Sometimes you just want a hamburger. But it will taste so much better if you make it with freshly ground beef and Jarlsberg cheese and slather Vermont butter on the toasted bun.

One of the secrets of good decorating is not to be afraid to be simple. Sometimes all you need is a jute rug from Pottery Barn.

The other secret is not to be afraid to make mistakes. It's part of the process. Things do go wrong. Sometimes a fabric doesn't look as great as you thought it would, or a paint color just doesn't look right in the light of that particular room. Don't linger on the mistake. Figure out a solution. If you can't live with it, redo it. I'm a great believer in the concept, Move on.

You can think you have everything planned down to the last nailhead, and still be blindsided. Once, in a screening room, we were constructing a wooden panel that slid up and down to cover a movie screen. We had the panel specially made to fit the dimensions of an antique Japanese screen we bought at Christie's and were planning to use on top of it. But when we finally received the screen, we realized the dimensions printed in the Christie's catalogue were wrong. What to do? We wound up wrapping the panel in straw, to add an interesting texture and camouflage the fact that the Japanese screen didn't quite fit. Luckily it worked.

Building a house is a bit like coordinating a rocket

I hung a painting over a mirror to extend the vista and at the same time expand the scale of the piece. The layering somehow turns it into both architecture and decoration. The sofa is a copy of an Italian original, upholstered in saddle leather. The Greco-Roman vases are reproductions as well, and create a sense of romance relatively inexpensively.

launch to the moon. There are so many things going on at any given moment that I'm actually surprised when things go smoothly. Mistakes come with the territory. The older I get, the more I realize that blame is often beside the point. It causes too much wear and tear on the situation. I simply reach into my pocket and pay for whatever it is to be redone.

When I first started working with Lynn de Rothschild on her New York apartment, she pointed to all this fancy molding that had been marbled and gilded and verdigrised and said, "I want to remove it." I said, "No, no, no. Let's just spray it white." I thought it would work. Thank God, I was right. Like any good gambler, I know my odds. If I guess wrong, I'm prepared to be accountable.

Sometimes I operate on instinct. But I've also learned that good ideas, and good design, can take time. I once asked my friend Guillaume Féau, who makes the most exquisite hand-carved boiserie in Paris, how long he had been in his location. "Two hundred years," he said. Now, that represents a wealth of history and tradition, a bred-in-the-bone knowledge of the craft that you just can't replicate easily. He knows boiserie. And you think you have a new idea? It's all been done before.

Two hundred years. It makes me feel as if I've barely begun, that all these things I've touched and handled and arranged so carefully are only of the moment. Eventually, all rooms get dispersed to the wind.

But I keep meeting with craftspeople, exploring what's possible, pushing the envelope. Guillaume has a room of stainless steel and tortoiseshell paneling originally made for Sao Schlumberger back in the 1970s. Very James Bond. I've been carrying around a photo of that room for months, wondering where I could use it. It's too good to pass up. I'm just waiting for the right basket.

An old found lantern, a carved ship's-hull plaque on the wall, and a reproduction end-grain American carpet give a sense of history and charm to a space that's virtually brand new. They contextualize the hall and make this house feel very much a part of Martha's Vineyard. Notice how the door is clipped. Architect Oscar Shamamian did that deliberately to make the house feel vaguely nautical and very shipshape.

The Houses

SANTA MONICA, CALIFORNIA

My friend Joe Roth was producing the Academy Awards one year and trying to look for a house. I immediately thought of one I'd admired for ages, which conveniently happened to be for sale. It's a very distinctive house, built in 1932 by Cedric Gibbons, the celebrated Hollywood art director, for his new wife, Dolores del Rio. Gibbons is also the man who designed the Oscar, so somehow it all seemed serendipitous. Joe never looked at another house. He loves movies, and this house is so cinematic.

Luckily it had been well taken care of, not ruined. All it needed was a little restorative work, and I tried to channel the spirit of the house whenever we made any alterations. From the outside, it's very Streamline Moderne. The façade is smooth, white, rectilinear. It almost looks like an ocean liner, docked amid the palm trees. There's a stainless steel front door, whose squared geometries ripple out onto the façade in wider and wider rectangles. Inside, it's even more like a movie set. Some

Above: Cedric Gibbons, the famed art director of Busby Berkeley musicals, as well as *The Wizard of Oz* and *An American in Paris*, designed his Streamline Moderne house in collaboration with architect Douglas Honnold. The rear façade is characterized by strong horizontal planes that cantilever out at one end like the prow of a ship. Large industrial-sash windows were part of the new machine-made aesthetic. Scott Frances / *Architectural Digest* © Condé Nast Publications Inc.

Opposite: The console at the foot of the stairs was custom-made for this house in a French 1930s style. It's metal, with a mirrored finish to reflect the light. The aluminum chair with Art Deco curves was designed by Warren McArthur, whose furniture was all the rage in 1930s Hollywood.

The built-in banquette is original to the house. I had it recovered in a caramel-colored silk and mohair blend—soft, with a bit of sleekness. The Art Deco patterns on the pillows were embroidered for me in Italy. The staircase leads up to the living room on the second floor.

of the principal rooms have this German submarine flooring—black rubber, incredibly glossy—which was originally used by Gibbons on the sets of the Busby Berkeley musicals because it was a seamless backdrop for the dancing girls.

You walk into a small sitting room, which we turned into more of a receiving room. Then there's a very dramatic, backlit staircase that was clearly designed for Dolores to sweep down dramatically and greet her guests. Then she would lead them up the stairs to a giant loft-like living room with mirrored and painted walls and all these floating and receding planes. It's about shape—straight lines and Art Deco curves—in this big white space. There's lots of built-in banquette seating and a big fireplace. I've seen publicity stills of Dolores in this room, in full evening dress dripping with diamonds. That's one vision, but you can take your pick. It's Fred Astaire and Ginger Rogers, any black-and-white Manhattan penthouse apartment out of a 1930s film, Katharine Hepburn in *Woman of the Year*, or *The Women*. We're talking a certain kind of glossy glamour.

Left: To make a large living room more manageable, I divided it into two major seating groups, separated by a big pedestal table in the center, opposite the fireplace. I love the way that stainless steel shelf, which functions as a mantel, just seems to float on its own, cutting right across the mirror. The stepped fireplace surround echoes the stepped ceiling— a visual leitmotif that continues throughout the house and sets up the strong geometries.
Scott Frances / *Architectural Digest* © Condé Nast Publications Inc.

Pages 79–80: The Donald Deskey table, in glass and chrome, is just the right size for an intimate supper for two. More could join in on the banquette. The two armchairs were designed by Paul Frankl, but only one is original. The other I had made for this house. The Danish candelabra—made of steel with cobalt blue and clear glass—is that one, unexpected hit of pure saturated color.
Scott Frances / *Architectural Digest* © Condé Nast Publications Inc.

The house was very beautiful, but very, very white. The architecture was almost pure line. Very graphic. But that can feel cold. I wanted to soften it a bit and make it more evocative and rich, by adding ivory, celadon, and camel tones. I covered the banquettes in the living room in several shades of mohair, from champagne to caramel. There's silk in the fiber, so it has a kind of sheen. Very fluid. Not hard. There are two long, low-ish bookcases, about five feet high, and I commissioned a pair of paintings in silver leaf and resin from Nancy Lorenz to hang over them. One represents day and the other, night.

Of course, even a black-and-white movie is not strictly black and white. There's a tremendous variety of shade and texture. I wanted that same kind of subtle palette. With the curtains drawn, the dining room takes on those sepia tones that you get in Hollywood film noir. It could have belonged to a character in a Raymond Chandler mystery. I pulled a lot of hand-woven silks and had fabrics especially embroidered for the house in Art Deco patterns. Yet it doesn't register as a lot of pattern or print. Just planes of solid, pale color.

The furnishings needed to have a sense of history.

I found a couple of period carpets and had a couple made. I bought quite a collection of Warren McArthur tubular metal furniture. We also made a number of pieces ourselves, like the big saddle-leather chairs. I found a half-circular Paul Evans chair and had it covered in suede. I didn't want to see wear and tear. I wanted the feel of a 1930s movie but I didn't want anything that was worn. None of that tawdry vintage look. The pieces had to be pristine, like that shiny black floor.

The kitchen is very sleek, with a new stainless steel island that I designed. It's a very modern aesthetic, celebrating the glory of the machine. In a way, the movies themselves are about a kind of artificial perfection, trying to remove the hand of man. Throughout the house, I used a lot of glass and silver and crystal, in simple shapes. I found original light fixtures from the 1930s with frosted glass shades.

Apparently Gibbons and del Rio each had their own separate floor, and her bedroom, which was clearly the master, did not have a shower. So I appropriated a piece of the closet and transformed it into a shower. It was a seamless addition that didn't compromise the archi-

I found the Art Deco dining table with a dark, glossy finish and the period chairs. The smoky mirrored screen adds a little mystery to the room. The carpet is a 1930s English design from Keshishian.

tectural integrity of the house. That was important to me because it's an important house from a historic standpoint. The bedroom is very simple and not terribly big, with pale celadon silk on the walls. The sleigh bed is based on a 1930s original and covered in parchment. Hanging black-and-white photography in this house seemed kind of a given, but I also chose some vibrantly colored contemporary paintings.

Del Rio was incredibly beautiful but apparently very high-maintenance, kind of like the house. Gibbons designed his own movie and cast it when he married her. He looked like a movie star himself, in his casually urbane clothes. Just the thing for a stroll in the garden, with its grid of pavers outlined in grass. The house is much more open in the back, with big industrial-sash windows. You walk out and descend down to the perfect swimming pool, com-

plete with poolhouse, tennis court, and archery range—where Errol Flynn was discovered, or so the story goes.

The level you have to hit as a designer in a house like this is pretty high. That black rubber floor really shows off everything, including dust. It's difficult to work with, because there's only so much you can do. You can't quite put a worn antique rug on this floor. It wouldn't have the vigor to survive. You need something with a certain sharpness or edge. Yet the black floor also acts as an incredibly strong platform for all the furniture.

I wanted the house to remind you of a beautiful black-and-white movie, but not a Miami hotel. That's the problem with Moderne. So many of the reference points are taken. But this has a whole other level of sophistication. It's silk charmeuse, cut on the bias—not a cozy family house. It's a super-glamorous set for living.

Above: One great Art Deco building deserves another, which is why Enoc Perez's painting of the Normandie Hotel in San Juan, Puerto Rico, is hanging in the master bedroom. The walls are covered in a celadon green Japanese silk from Donghia. The torchère was designed by Jacques Adnet in 1930.
Scott Frances / *Architectural Digest* © Condé Nast Publications Inc.

Opposite: A new bathroom added to the poolhouse repeats the same vocabulary—the stepped ceiling, the porthole window—found in the main house. We did substitute black terrazzo for the black rubber, German submarine flooring.

CARBON BEACH, CALIFORNIA

The light at the beach is reason enough to live there. There's the hazy neon light of early morning, the scorching rays at noon, the honeyed afternoon light that turns everything golden. And then there are those gray, overcast days when the fog rolls in. Having grown up at the beach, I know just how cold and damp it can get, even in summer. So I'm always trying to create an interior that feels cozy yet reductive. No clutter. I don't want to distract from the beauty of the ocean.

I could do a blue-and-white-striped beach house in my sleep, so I wanted something a little different for this house in Malibu, designed by architect Lewin Wertheimer. I love texture rather than plain painted walls, so I used a wallpaper by Elizabeth Dow in the living room. It's a lovely pale blue that has been cross-hatched to reveal the

ivory underneath, which gives it a sense of depth and creates a pretty play of light. The furnishings are relatively spare—a sofa, two chairs. The antique Oushak rug adds a certain softness. The simple mirror over the fireplace is from my Jasper collection.

It's always a battle for the designer to get everything done, down to the last pillow, before the clients move in. But there are certain things you cannot plan. I found that beautiful painted cupboard in Sweden when the project was almost done, and put it in at the last minute. It looks like a column, with its own little capital on top, and has a calm, sculptural presence that anchors the room.

The furniture in the dining room has a different kind of weight and sophistication. The cupboard in there is Dutch, and looks like a building all by itself.

Above: The porch out back is the kind of place where once you sit down, you never want to get up. It runs the length of the house, and I furnished it with simple outdoor furniture that fits right in with the simple architecture of the house. The sturdy Weatherend chaises and chairs are covered in Perennials outdoor fabric.

Opposite: The Shingle-style house was designed by architect Lewin Wertheimer, who got the proportions right and paid close attention to the details. I like the fact that when you open the front door, you see straight through to the ocean.

My impulse out at the beach is to clear away the clutter and focus on the sky and the sea. The living room is done in soft muted colors—a blue-green on the sofa, a sage stripe on the chairs. The weathered, painted cabinet has the presence of a piece of sculpture and embodies the grace and purity of Swedish style. I designed the Duke mirror above the mantel for my Jasper collection.

It's a massive piece, hand-carved of ebony and palisander back in the seventeenth century. The dining table is English and was made in 1850. But the piece that really transforms the room is the lantern, a copy of a late eighteenth-century Strawberry Hill Gothic chinoiserie original. It's got that great, crazy scale, and it's less serious than a chandelier. I think a lantern just works better in a beach house. In fact, if you want to change the mood of any room, just put a lantern in it.

Everybody feels comfortable in this house. The rooms are a good size, the proportions are right. The architecture is simple and reductive, and I didn't want to mess that up by adding too much. The fabrics—linen, chintz, ticking stripes—will never go out of style. I think that kind of familiarity accelerates your ability to relax. The master bedroom has a tremendous amount of window, and the curtains are made from a chintz I designed for Cowtan & Tout. When it's not sunny out, you can pull them closed and be enveloped in flowers. The pattern is based on a document I found in England, probably from the 1860s. It's a classic, drowsy floral chintz. I just changed the coloring a bit to make it more cheerful. I love antique textiles. If you can't get the real thing, you can always find something that has an antique quality. It's hard to get a king-sized bed to look right, but the reductive Shaker four-poster helps. The bench at the foot of the bed is actually a pop-up TV cabinet. Instead of the usual botanicals, I hung Indian miniatures on the wall.

Every room deserves one dramatic element. The big round mirror in the master bath looks like a pocket watch on steroids. It's flanked by a pair of sconces. No overhead lights. I try to discourage overhead lights because they're so unflattering. They fill a space with uniform light and remove any charm or nuance. I prefer quiet pools of light, from lamps.

The guest room was in desperate need of something to make it magical. It was too small for a draped bed, so I draped the room itself in my Moghul Panel fabric, and found the Sri Lankan four-poster. I couldn't let the invention stop with the kitchen. I've been playing around with the classic American kitchen for years, trying to come up with something different. The island here is made of ebonized wood in the style of the Aesthetic Movement. It has a simple soapstone top. There's a traditional farmhouse sink under the window. Open cupboards add a sense of informality, and they're also practical. In a beach house where you don't live year-round, it's easier when the shelves are open because you don't have to remember where everything is kept. I painted the walls a blue-green to create a little contrast with the khaki cabinets.

Remember those paper lanterns that people used to string up for a party? As soon as you saw them, you felt festive. The nineteenth-century Chinese light fixtures in this kitchen have the same charm. They're the unexpected note that makes a room memorable.

Opposite: Just a few pieces, but each has big, bold scale—that's what makes this dining room interesting. The magnificent copper chinoiserie lantern, from Soane in London, catches the eye first. It's strong enough to hold its own against the stately c. 1650 Dutch cupboard. The James chairs, upholstered in a linen stripe by Clarence House, are my version of country Chippendale and were designed for my Jasper collection. The blanc de chine vases and jars are from J. F. Chen.

Above: Turquoise-blue decanters from India add a touch of color.

Above: With a farmhouse sink, plate racks, and open shelves, this looks like a simple cottage kitchen. But then the Chinese lanterns and the island—made of ebonized wood and soapstone in the style of the Aesthetic Movement—take it in a surprising, more sophisticated direction. The Newport bar chair is by Charles Fradin.

Opposite: In the study, the George wing chair I designed for Jasper is upholstered in my Saratoga leather in olive, designed for Cowtan & Tout. Bennison's Zanzibar chintz covers the custom sofa. A reading alcove with a window seat doubles as an extra guest room.

Opposite: In the master bedroom, I designed a Shaker-style four-poster king-sized bed, which I oriented toward the view. At its foot is a pop-up TV cabinet disguised as a bench. The chandelier is Venetian glass. The curtain fabric is Carlyle, the quintessentially English chintz I designed for Cowtan & Tout.

Above: In a small guest room, I created a sense of drama by wrapping all four walls in my Indian Moghul Panels. I found the Sri Lankan shell bed at Suzanne Hollis. The pillows embroidered with gold metallic thread come from Sumatra and date to the 1920s.

MALIBU, CALIFORNIA

I've designed several houses for Cindy Crawford, who has been my friend for a very long time. But this was the first I did for her and Rande Gerber after they got married, and I think it's a fusion of their two styles. Rande has created all these nightclubs and bars and likes ceremony and drama. Cindy's taste is more pragmatic and traditional. The house is really about bringing those two impulses together.

They decided they wanted to live in Malibu and found an amazing site. The property starts at the road and then steps down to the ocean in a series of terraces. Architect Oscar Shamamian developed the plan, which is actually five buildings—one at the gate, one at the ocean, and in between is the main house, a gym, and an office. As soon as you arrive, there's a strong ceremonial element—you cross a bridge over a shallow pool of water to get to the temple-like front door—which is very Rande. Then inside are all the things a family needs—beautiful

Above: This is not the typical Malibu beach house, a fact that becomes clear as soon as you open the gate. A bridge spans a shallow pool of water and you have to walk across it to get to the front door, which is flanked with hand-carved mahogany panels from Morocco. The atmosphere feels more like Southeast Asia than Southern California.

Opposite: The house, designed by Oscar Shamamian, is terraced into a cliff overlooking the ocean. You can walk down to the private beach or jump into the infinity pool or sink into the Jacuzzi. Rios Clementi Hale Studios did the landscape design.

bedrooms, practical baths, a playroom for the children—very warm and comfortable, like Cindy.

Both of them love Bali, and the vision is a little Balinese, a little Japanese. It reminds me of the kind of houses you see in old photographs of rural hill stations in India or the Philippines. Dark wood, white walls, bamboo matting, and bamboo shades. It has a kind of English Colonial sensibility, but it's not a deliberate re-creation, more Anywhere Colonial. Once in a while, I think about having a house photographed in black-and-white, just to see what it would look like. This house would have a kind of historic quality. Yet it feels very hip and modern at the same time.

As soon as you step into the entrance hall, which is two stories high, you can see straight through to the ocean. There's a carved settee from Senegal and bookcases lit by alabaster lamps. The ceiling gets lower as you walk through the hall. You're compressed—a trick utilized by Frank Lloyd Wright to make the next room feel even larger—and then you emerge into this big expansive space, with the family room and kitchen on one side and the dining room on the other. At the far end of the hall is this amazing

Left: When you step into the house, you can see straight through to the Pacific. The series of rooms is processional, and the temple-like feeling is reinforced by the wooden beams over each doorway. There's a Moroccan wool rug on the floor, which is more modern and reductive than a traditional Oriental. I found the 1850s Chinese bookcase in Belgium and the nineteenth-century Chinese black lacquer scroll table in Los Angeles, at J. F. Chen.

Above: The family room, open to the kitchen, is comfortable and unpretentious. The Bond Street sofa by Donghia is upholstered in a deep indigo-blue cotton-linen print by John Robshaw. There's something about blue that's very soothing to the eye. I covered the ceiling with grass cloth and added ceiling fans to accentuate the tropical ambience.

pedestal table Cindy and I bought in London ten years ago, made of a four-inch-thick piece of Egyptian alabaster on a blackened oak base. It looks very European Grand Tour, but then it's surrounded by lanterns and an Anglo-Indian chair, which makes the whole place feel more like a plantation in the tropics. I think a center hall table is a very practical concept. It's a place to drop keys, mail, a sweater you don't want to forget, books. A major piece of furniture like this also creates a focal point at the end of a series of rooms. When the sunlight is pouring in, all you see is the outline of the table against the brightness. It's a very sculptural piece that anchors the space.

In Malibu, the boundaries between inside and out are blurred. Many of the walls are actually pocket doors, so you can push them aside and dissolve the wall, opening the whole room to the outdoors. The furniture is strong and simple—custom-made teak sofas, rattan lounge chairs, Moroccan rugs. The colors are strong and simple, too, almost primitive—madder red, indigo blue—in hand-blocked Indian cottons from John Robshaw or Thai silks. Even when they fade in the sun,

Above: A fireplace in a dining room is a great asset, and I papered the ceiling in white-gold leaf to catch the flickering light. I found the unusual British copper ball lantern, c. 1820, at Ann-Morris Antiques. The chairs are based on a Moroccan original, which I had copied. The painting is by Nancy Lorenz.

Opposite: A strong piece of furniture, like this table topped with Egyptian alabaster, acts as an anchor in a room. Here it also marks the end point of the central axis of the house. I think there should always be something interesting to see at the end of a hallway. The Anglo-Indian armchair dates from the 1860s and is from Ann-Morris Antiques.

they will still be beautiful. Everything has a real texture. There is no filler, no pale little prints. If a fabric is not interesting on the bolt, I won't use it. I tend to pick a lot of strong patterns, and then they all work well together because they're all at the same volume. There's nothing recessive. Every fabric counts.

When I was just starting out, I worked for an old-line firm that was the zenith of suburban decorating. Every bed skirt was cotton taffeta. For each room, you found a big print, a small print, and then a texture that worked with it. That just never interested me at all. There's no strong idea. I hate fabrics that are badly drawn and badly printed. If it's not hand-blocked—and there are so few left—it has to look hand-blocked. Right now, I'm having a chintz made from a document I found, and there are something like twenty colors in it. Hand-printing that will not be easy, but it's worth it.

Yet it's not about rarity or price. I'd rather have a $9-a-yard Belgian linen than a badly made $100-a-yard silk. I have no qualms about buying printed cotton bedspreads at Urban Outfitters if they have that vibration I'm looking for. One of the greatest excitements of my life was finding these simple Indonesian wastebaskets that I love,

Left: In the pool cabana, the boundaries between inside and out seem to dissolve. The rattan armchairs are made by Bielecky Brothers. I bought the nineteenth-century Chinese lantern at auction and kept the theme going with a Ming coffee table I designed myself.

Above: Formality is not a word that applies to this family. The living room is just as casual and inviting as the rest of the house. I had the teak sofas custom-made and upholstered them in Jim Thompson's Thai Silk IV. The paired coffee tables are by Charles Jacobsen. Bamboo matting covers the floor.

made of straw with black detailing woven into them. They are as beautiful to me as a million-dollar Oriental rug.

Cindy and Rande understand that. Each object we brought into the house has integrity. Their home is all about being comfortable, about putting people at ease. The sofas were chosen for comfort. Chairs swivel. The deep indigo blue cotton on the furniture in the family room is very soothing to the eye and offers a retreat from the bright sun. Then, when the view disappears at night, the rich colors and the dark woods hold the room together and make it feel warm. We put Hawaiian matting made of woven straw on the ceiling—a very simple and inexpensive idea, yet it gives a beautiful lid to the room. Ceilings are often forgotten. The matting is one of those subtle details that creates instant atmosphere.

Above: This, to me, is the ultimate British Colonial bathroom. There's nothing more classic than marble-topped mahogany, and there's a sense of history to the fixtures. The sink, tub, and faucets are all part of my Town collection for Kallista.

Right: The master bedroom is soft and simple, both feminine and masculine at the same time. The rugs were made by the Beni Ouarain tribe in Morocco and I chose them for their pattern and texture—strong, yet subtle. The curtains are creamy linen from Travers. I think this room, with its pale white walls and peaked roof, feels slightly more ethereal than the rest of the house, which is more earthy and grounded.

Opposite: I love hand-blocked fabrics, like those made by John Robshaw, and used them for the coverlet and the pillow shams in a guest room. The rope bed is by John Himmel and the bedside table next to it is my own design.

Above: Another guest room is furnished with an Indian inlaid chest and an Indian bed and a seventeenth-century–style French chair upholstered in old Fortuny. The casement window lets in the breeze and has a wonderful view up the coast.

MILLBROOK, NEW YORK

In my work, I'm always trying to create a sense of place. My clients, the television director James Burrows and his wife Debbie, fell in love with this property in Millbrook, New York. There's a sweep to the land, with forever views of rolling hills and the most idyllic country-side. Now architect Gil Schafer and I needed to build a house that lived up to the site. We took a close look at the local vernacular and designed a late eighteenth-century Colonial with higher ceilings and all the modern conveniences. It's a brand-new house that looks old because it

actually has old components. We bought an old house near Hudson, New York, and took it apart and salvaged the pieces. We recycled the beams and the floors and the moldings. We bought incredible nineteenth-century wallpaper panels at auction and found beautiful old chimneypieces. It's difficult sometimes to stay true to a theme and not get too fancy, but I think we succeeded. This definitely feels like a big, rambling upstate New York country house.

It's a classic center-hall plan. From the front door, you can see right through to the view. In the dining

Above: This is a center-hall Colonial, furnished in the classic way with a handsome Georgian mahogany bookcase and two beautifully shaped hall chairs. Old wide floorboards and walls covered in a sandy Venetian plaster give the newly built house a sense of age.

Opposite: Quintessentially American furniture—a wicker sofa, a Windsor chair, an old farm table with a scrubbed wood top—gives the sunroom a simple country charm. An antique French game box is used as a coffee table. Porch ceilings are traditionally painted blue—at one point it was thought to ward off bugs—and I followed that old custom here. An antique ceiling fan creates a nice breeze.

room, we had a mural painted, depicting the surrounding countryside. It looks antique, almost as if it has a kind of sepia tint. There's some color, just not a lot. All through the house, we tried to buy things that already had a patina. We wanted that sense of being slightly worn, as opposed to overly polished. The dining table is English, probably late eighteenth century, a long rectangle with rounded corners. The wood is absolutely beautiful. When you wax something for over a hundred years, it brings out the character. That's something you can never duplicate from scratch, no matter how hard you try. The dining chairs are covered in bright red tufted leather. French doors open onto a long covered porch that runs the length of the house and overlooks the valley.

We designed the drawing room as a double parlor, each half organized around a fireplace that became the focus of a seating arrangement. The furniture is English, in country-house condition, which implies that the house has a history and was not furnished straight out of the showroom. One Regency sofa is real, the other is a copy. The colors in the Sultanabad carpets have become muted over the years. In the library, bookshelves line the walls from floor to ceiling. The vintage baby grand belonged to James's father, Abe Burrows, who wrote and directed Broadway musicals.

The big family kitchen is commensurate with the scale of the house. Flamed granite countertops have a rough, worn texture. Shadowy colors sponge up the light and give the house a sense of age. No white is white. No wall is flat. The sun moves around the rooms and picks out various details, like the carved moldings.

In the sun porch, comfy rattan chairs are gathered around a big square coffee table. There's an old stone fireplace and an antique ceiling fan. The fact that we could have high ceilings allowed us to create all these beautiful volumes. The room is lofty. You can almost feel the breeze.

Debbie had always wanted a bedroom with Chinese wallpaper, so I had this beautiful eighteenth-century

---

We conceived of this project as a gentleman's farmhouse, which means no crystal chandelier in the dining room. Instead, I chose a nineteenth-century billiard fixture—less fancy and more masculine. The eighteenth-century portrait of Henry Hudson over the mantel was bought at auction. The dining chairs are English, dating from the 1860s. Inspired by the traditional red hunting jacket, I upholstered them in red leather.

Above: This is one of two major seating groups, each centered around a fireplace, in the large, double-parlor drawing room. Both the linen damask on the sofa and my Bentley Rose chintz, used for the curtains, have a lovely antique quality that makes the room feel as if it's been around for a while.

Opposite: The sofa in the library is upholstered in a linen velvet from my Jasper collection, in the same warm wheat color as the blanket-soft wool from Colefax & Fowler used for the curtains. The easy chair is covered in my Montecatini fabric for Cowtan & Tout. I found the faux-bamboo antique library ladder in Hudson, New York.

Chinese wallpaper copied for the walls in the master suite. The graceful arches and the fireplace were salvaged from the old Hudson house. The colors are pale blues and creams, very restful. Each bedroom is unique. We personalized them with these extraordinary wallpapers from Adelphi Paper Hangings, a workshop that still makes wallpaper the old-fashioned way. That means each is printed by hand, on thick matte paper. They feel softer, older. The patterns are reproductions of early eighteenth- and nineteenth-century American wallpapers. They have a kind of bold, quirky charm that really helps a new room.

Each bedroom has a four-poster bed and a dressing room and a bathroom—some with tubs, some with showers—but all with real furniture. It's amazing how different a bathroom can feel once you put a table in there, with a lamp. Suddenly it seems cozy and much more antique.

Throughout the house, all the old wood and the old mantels and the old hardware add up to character. They provide patina and that little touch of eccentricity. That's what makes this house feel as if it has been around forever. It's all an illusion, but it works. The house feels authentic and true to this place.

Opposite: The countertops in the kitchen are made of flamed granite, which looks more soft and worn than polished granite and happens to be very durable. The pot rack was custom-made for me by Ann-Morris Antiques.

Above: This early nineteenth-century wallpaper was crumbling when I bought it at auction. We reinstalled it in the mudroom, which is furnished with a little desk—a copy of an Edwardian original made by Ann-Morris Antiques.

Opposite: Pocket doors in a lovely archway, salvaged from an old country house, separate the bedroom from the sitting room in the master suite. I found a pair of eighteenth-century English posts and made a simple canopy bed, hung in creamy linen.

Above: The sofa in the sitting room is covered in my linen ticking stripe, with my Indian Flower hemp on the pillows. I wanted all the fabrics to be soft and summery, as if everything had faded a bit in the sun over the years. The wallpaper that connects the two rooms was made for me by de Gournay.

Opposite: This guest room is quite simple and severe in black and cream, with a new Hepplewhite-style bed in an ebony finish. Nothing in this room looks fussy or decorated. The chest at the foot of the bed is a very rare piece that was made in the Bahamas. The quilt is a patchwork of old English chintzes.

Above: This is a play on the classic stripe you often see in early American houses, handmade for me in a wallpaper by Elizabeth Dow. The tub and faucets are from the collection I did for Kallista. I love that sweet little hourglass-shaped chair, which has followed the clients around from one house to another. It's too good to give up.

SANTA BARBARA, CALIFORNIA

There are a lot of Italianate houses in Santa Barbara, but often they look a little too new. The idea here was to build a classic Italianate house and give it the kind of patina it would have had naturally, if it had been built a century or two ago.

The house, designed by the architect Don Nulty, is basically a pavilion flanked by two wings. The front door opens into a long hall, paved in terra cotta tile and lit by lanterns and wrought-iron sconces. Lighting plays a large part in creating atmosphere, and I deliberately

chose a diverse vocabulary of fixtures for the house. Most were custom-made and specially finished, which creates this interesting, eccentric mix. If the lighting is too uniform and consistent, a house looks modern and the illusion is spoiled.

The long hall leads to a majestic living room with a beamed ceiling that's twenty feet high. You can't put a conventional mantelpiece in a room like this. It would be dwarfed. I found a large, early seventeenth-century chimneypiece that looks like it came out of a castle and really

Above: This Santa Barbara house feels like the kind of Mediterranean villa you might see on the shores of Lake Como. The central pavilion is almost more glass than wall, with three large arched windows that open onto an expansive terrace overlooking the garden out back.

Opposite: The lanterns hanging from the vaulted ceiling in the entrance hall are reproductions of old Italian pieces. A decorative trompe l'oeil painting over the door to the dining room adds a sense of age and grandeur to a new house. Two Khotan rugs warm up the tiled floor. Near a seventeenth-century Tuscan table, a pair of Indonesian plant stands flank the doors to the terrace.

sets the tone. The octagonal mirror above it, made of ebonized wood and brass, is on the same scale. It reflects the light and relieves the mass of the chimneypiece. Venetian plaster on the walls gives the room a sense of texture and age. The decorative painting at the cornice line is the kind of thing you might see in an old Italian villa. We used a lot of decorative painting on the walls, the ceilings, and the overdoors to make the house feel as if it had more weight and character.

The furniture arrangement in the living room is divided into two separate groupings, one by the fireplace and one oriented to the giant cabinet that anchors the other side of the room. The two groups help break up the space, so the room doesn't feel quite so big. It's comfortable for two people, or twenty. The Sultanabad carpet, in lovely muted blues and reds, sets up the palette, which teeters between those two colors. If it were too blue, the room would feel too cool. If it were too red, it could turn into an Italian restaurant. This way, it's balanced between

blue and red, which creates just the right level of warmth. I wanted very solid, comfortable pieces of furniture. The architecture is very weighty, so the furniture had to feel equally substantial. Yet I didn't want it to become monolithic. That's why the blue velvet on the sofa has a lot of pattern. Otherwise, it could feel like a big blue block.

You need a little lightness to create a balance between heavy and light pieces, which is why so many tables have lovely turned legs. The side table in dark, ebonized wood with an inlaid marble top adds a little exoticism. A variety of styles is a shorthand way to convey a sense of history, as if the furniture had been collected over generations rather than bought all at once. The coffee table is a reproduction of a Portuguese piece and has its own diamond-patterned inlay on top. The huge Tuscan storage cabinet probably came out of a monastery or a convent, and has just the right proportions for the room. A massive piece like that, which feels as if it has been here forever, adds instant age and grandeur to a room.

Opposite: The living room must be twenty feet high, so the chimneypiece needed to be tall as well to break up the height and help bring the room down to human scale. The beamed ceiling and the decorative painting at the cornice line enhance the sense of age. I like all those lovely curved legs on the side table, which is a reproduction of a Chinese lacquer original.

Above: I can't resist a beautiful glaze. This simple little Chinese export pot is filled with orchids.

I put an Italian refectory table behind the blue sofa. It creates a strong horizontal to counter the verticals of the tall arched windows and doors, and also defines the passage between the two seating areas. In a way, the lamp on top of the table becomes the centerpiece of the room and helps bring the whole space down to human scale.

In the dining room, I had an artist paint this mysterious, misty mural of a landscape with trees and hills. Dining rooms are always tough. You want to create a sense of magic, and I think nothing does it better than a mural. Suddenly you're enveloped in this otherworldly atmosphere. You're looking beyond the walls to the trees and sky. Reality blurs. The very air in the room seems soft and shadowy, like twilight.

The mood may be dreamy but the furniture has to be completely functional. We had the dining table and the chairs custom-made in that cool, elegant Northern Italian style. The damask-like fabric on the chairs is linen, as opposed to silk. The table is very practical. It can be expanded, depending on the number of guests. The console against the wall is a big antique Italian piece, higher than normal, which suits the proportions of the room. Above it, I hung a Neoclassical Italian mirror that picks up the gold in the chairs. The collection of blue-and-white Chinese porcelain brings in an element of color and counteracts the intensely masculine quality of the console. The curve of the porcelain, and its delicacy, feels more feminine. There's a nice balance of shape and color. Red would have been a little too hectic for this room. Blue is more meditative and calming.

For the master bedroom, I found this beautiful Mallorcan-style bed that reads as pure, sculptural form. It has these unusual turned posts made of ebonized wood. Very strong, and perfect for the house because it's romantic

---

Above: This is another composition about dark and light, shape and texture. A collection of Chinese axe blades is grouped on a stone-topped table, next to a carved-wood lamp and a plaster urn. I bought the antique Italian mirror, one of a pair, at auction.

Opposite: It's hard to convey any sense of romance or style with upholstered furniture alone, which is why you need the contrast of wood pieces like those tables with interesting Mediterranean-style turned legs. The chandeliers, made in Italy and strung with wood and glass beads, have the right volume but also a certain lightness. The lamp on the center table, made out of a giant Imari vase, keeps up with the scale of the room.

Opposite: A collection of blue-and-white porcelain gives this dining room a more eclectic, slightly exotic feeling. I like the way you can mix all sorts of blue and white objects and they will always work together. The yellows and sepias in the mural are fairly warm, and the blue and white acts as a device to cool it down visually and add a sense of crispness. If everything in the room were the same color as the walls, it could get a bit murky.

Above: A handpainted mural gives the room a whole other atmosphere, transporting you to another space and time. The landscape seems to be seen through a mist. It's poetic and evocative. Things like murals and antique mirrors can take an ordinary room and make it magical.

and yet there's a real weight to it. I hung a pretty embroidered fabric from Chelsea Textiles just at the head of the
bed, to add a little softness. The settee at the foot of the
bed is Italian, covered with a lovely rustic raw silk stenciled
in soft muted colors. It's a very practical piece. You can
throw a blanket on it, or sit and talk. I think there should
always be another place to sit in a bedroom besides the
bed. The rug is a faded Tabriz in grays, blues, and a soft
Sienna yellow that we picked up and mixed into the
Venetian plaster on the walls. On one wall, I hung a
leather screen, almost as if it were a painting. It's early
eighteenth-century Dutch, gilded and painted with a

very strong, powerful pattern. It adds texture and
dimension to the space. So does the cast-plaster motif
on the ceiling, which reinforces the sense of age and
finishes off the room.

The outdoor spaces in this particular house are just
as comfortable and varied as the interiors. Santa Barbara
has this remarkable climate. It's never too hot or too
cold, which means you can live outside all year round.
We created several outdoor living rooms overlooking the
garden and the views, complete with outdoor fireplaces.
There's something wonderful about gathering around a
cozy fire under the stars.

Above: It's interesting how hanging an eighteenth-century Dutch painted-leather screen on the wall changes your perception of it. Suddenly the piece is more like an art object. I love the way it adds so much texture to the space. The beautifully carved antique mirror by the door is a little jewel, made in Italy.

Opposite: Architect Don Nulty chose the cast-plaster motif on the ceiling, which is the kind of thing you might see at the Alhambra palace in Spain. The unusual posts on the bed bring in more of that Mediterranean influence. The raw silk on the Italian settee is by Travers and the blue woven fabric on the pillows is by Rose Tarlow.

Above: All of the parties at this house seem to end up with everyone sitting around the outdoor fireplace. I hung a sandstone window from India over the mantel. The wicker sofa and chairs are upholstered in a Rose Tarlow fabric. The coffee table is topped in stone, which is impervious to the weather.

Opposite: The Janus et Cie chaises by the pool are covered in a Perennials outdoor stripe that reminds me of the French Riviera. Just below the dining terrace, under that carved stone arch, is a fountain that can be heard on the terrace and by the pool.

LONDON, ENGLAND

Longtime friends and clients decided, after their children had left the nest, that they wanted to spend more time in London. So I went off with various real estate brokers and looked at atrocity after atrocity, the relics of a recent speculative frenzy when everybody pulled down centuries-old moldings and replaced them with slick white walls. Anything cozy and great, from Nancy Lancaster to Syrie Maugham, had been washed away in a sea of dark bamboo flooring and white sectional sofas. It was London as perpetual bachelor pad.

That's a problem, because in a distinguished neighborhood like Belgravia, where my clients wanted to live, "groovy" doesn't really work. It always looks slightly sinister, like a set for a Harold Pinter play. So I kept searching. Being, of course, a great lover of cross-referencing, I pulled in every resource available to me to aid in the pursuit, from the pages of *Country Life* magazine to primelocation.com. I quizzed my dinner companions. Then, at the very end of the very last day, one broker showed me this incredible apartment on Eaton Square.

Above: The entrance hall of this palatial London townhouse is filled with an eclectic assortment of objects that announce, Here is the home of a serious collector. The abstract painting over the staircase is by French artist Pierre Soulages. It's quite a contrast to the other, more traditional paintings in the room, but that's what creates energy.

Opposite: An eighteenth-century Japanese lacquered cabinet provides a focal point at the end of a hallway. On top of it, I arranged a white porcelain Chinese vase, a drawing by David Bomberg, and a custom-made bronze uplight that casts interesting shadows.

Pages 133–34: A stunning nineteenth-century painting by French artist Leon Bonnat, in a size suited to the Louvre, dominates the entrance hall. Somehow, by putting a leather sofa underneath we managed to domesticate it. I hung a French Régence mirror over a French Empire cabinet. The rug is a Sultanabad.

It belonged to a couple who had spent ten years putting together a number of flats, until they had the drawing room floors of three contiguous houses—ninety lateral feet overlooking the square—plus an upper and lower floor. I brought my clients to see it, and they turned to me and said, "That's it."

The architecture was superb, and thankfully a previous renovation had been done quite well. The entrance hall was covered in stucco, scored to look like big slabs of stone. Very classical. Already, that plays with our perception, and I decided to hang a huge, huge, huge nineteenth-century academic painting, which fills a whole wall and really energizes the space. It's a portrait of Samson wrestling with a lion. It must be eleven feet high. It's like a window in this windowless room and it extends the space dramatically. Underneath it is a long leather sofa. A hall sofa always gives me the sense that I'm in an English country house. Then I added a Louis XVI cabinet, a French Empire cabinet, a French Regency mirror, a Chinese bowl in an ormolu mount, a tall Chinese pot on the floor. On the wall over the staircase I hung a giant 1960s painting by the French artist Pierre Soulages—big brushstrokes in caramel and black, very dramatic. All these strong, large-scale elements basically pull you through the space as your eye goes from one to the other, masking the fact that the hall is not actually that big. And then the Soulages pulls you upstairs.

It's an eccentric mix, and it started with a vision—Gianni Agnelli in London. What would a wealthy Italian living in London surround himself with? He would take the best of Europe—all eras, all styles—and put them together. He would not be bound by convention. There would be a touch of the exotic. And the modern painting announces a certain European jet-set glamour, almost a James Bond kind of allure. As a teenager, I was always obsessed by James Bond movies and the James Bond aesthetic, but I related even more to the aesthetic of the villian. Bond villains were incredibly sophisticated. They always had a much better idea of how to live.

This apartment is on one of the most beautiful squares in London, and it represents everything I love about English decorating, which consists of much more than flowery chintz. Look at the diversity of John Fowler's work, which could be astonishingly modern. The apartment he did for Pauline de Rothschild at the Albany, with that incredible French iron bed in the middle of the room, was so reductive and refined. Timeless. His own house, the Hunting Lodge, was all about charm. The pieces he found and put together are not the kind of thing you can pick up at a furniture showroom. You have to hunt for them. When I'm buying furniture, the phrase I love to hear is "country-house condition," which is auction terminology for something that's been knocked around a bit. It means it has some patina and has not been over-restored. That's the kind of furniture you see in an English country house. The first thing people say about English decorating is that it's comfortable. The second is that it's pretty, and there's nothing wrong with pretty, by the way. John Fowler's rooms were always very pretty. Pretty is a much-maligned term.

This drawing room is pretty. It's also the most classical room in the apartment. The plaster ceiling is original, and we put a very pale yellow Venetian plaster on the walls. The scheme started with that incredible Indian carpet, a very rare, early Agra with an unusual medallion pattern. I knew it was amazing as soon as I saw it in the auction catalog. I was buying wine in Mallorca when my cell phone rang and it was Sotheby's, to let me know the bidding had started. I stepped out onto the cobbled street and just kept saying, "Go, go, keep going," until it was mine. Later I found out that all these dealers I really respect were also bidding on it. I also bought that magnificent pair of girandole mirrors, with eagles on top, at auction. Hard to use because they're seven feet high, but given the proportions of this room, they fit perfectly. They're hung over a pair of French commodes with Boulle-like detailing, bought when Partridge's, a grand old English furniture shop on Bond Street, sold off a few of their things. I set a Tang

Pages 135–36: In the drawing room, I took out a 1940s black Italian mantel—a recent addition—and replaced it with a Georgian mantel that looks original to the house. I had the two cabinets made for me in Russia when I couldn't find anything antique with the proper scale. The desk is French, in the style of Boulle, with tortoiseshell and brass detailing. Flanking it are two stately armchairs, found at the Steinitz Gallery in Paris and already upholstered in that lovely old Genoese silk velvet.

Opposite: I doubt I will ever see a more magnificent pair of Georgian girandoles than these, seven feet high and crowned with eagles. Chinese Tang horses stand facing each other on a pair of lacquered commodes. The sofa with a scalloped back was inspired by a Florentine original and is upholstered in a ribbed Ottoman silk. Antique and new pillows in purple and blue pull out some of the colors in the super-rare nineteenth-century Indian carpet. Then I added that red crack-lacquer coffee table in a French 1960s-style which is a dissonant not that takes the room in another direction for a moment and makes it memorable.

horse on each commode. My associate was worried they'd be too big, but I knew they were going to be fine. I'm a big believer in big scale. There are not that many pieces in this room, but each is substantial. I think that gives the room a sense of grandeur.

The sofa and chairs have very strong, traditional shapes, yet the colors are a little unexpected—an absinthe-colored silk, a celadon damask, an amber silk velvet. The curtains are a beautiful teal-blue vertical stripe. You want the eye to go up, to appreciate the height of the windows. If I had used a floral, the room would have lost a certain masculine strength. That shade of blue doesn't reappear in any of the other fabrics because that kind of matching seems almost corny to me. It's much more interesting to make things relate in other ways, such as texture or shape. I like to pick things as I go, and gradually carve out the coloration of a room, instead of deciding on everything all at once. I usually leave a few deliberate blanks, to fill in later. If you're rushed to pull the trigger, it's hard to get this kind of complexity. Decorating is like a three-dimensional chess game. Sometimes you make a spontaneous move and it turns out to be great. Other times, a room needs a bit of adjusting, to be a better fit for the clients. If a sofa doesn't work, I take it out and replace it. You have to be willing to live dangerously, because often the best ideas are only discovered at the end. A lamp I find at the last minute can completely alter a room.

I pay attention to negative space as much as positive space, and try to understand the way furniture interacts. Being open to change is a really good thing. That contemporary coffee table isn't the most obvious choice for this room. It's French 1960s-style and so red! Yet it works, and happens to be exactly the right size. I really wanted Russian cabinets for the walls on either side of the fireplace, but couldn't find the right size in an antique. So I had them made, in Russia. One day they'll move out, if I find something better. I'm still searching for the right chandelier.

There are only a few paintings in the room, but they have great presence. Joseph Wright of Derby, the eighteenth-century English portrait painter, did the large

---

Pages 139–40: There's something compelling about the juxtaposition of that nineteenth-century English mirror and those Hispano-Moroccan tiles, hung over the fireplace in the library. It suggests a breadth of knowledge and interest on the part of the collector who has put together all these extraordinary objects from different cultures. The bronze statue in the window of Louis XIV on horseback is a nineteenth-century copy of a much larger piece. The library table doubles as a dining table. The chairs are upholstered in a silk velvet from my Jasper collection.

Left: In a dark paneled library, the bright saffron-colored silk curtains at the windows come as a delightful surprise. I pulled in more color on the sofa with the pillows, made from one of my favorite silk plaids from Le Manach in Paris, a red-and-white Turkish ikat, and more saffron silk. Like the bright turquoise Chinese vase, they keep a dark room from getting too ponderous. The lamps in the background, from Mallett, are made from red Berlin pottery. Everything in this room feels worthy of a museum.

painting of an underwater grotto in Salerno, Italy. It's all shadow and light, and forms another powerful shape—like a giant oculus—in the space. Then I found these wonderful eighteenth-century School of Rome paintings and couldn't figure out what to do with them. So I said, "Let's put them over the doors." It's an unexpected take on the traditional overdoor, and they make a tall room seem even taller.

In the library, the mood changes a bit and becomes more exotic. After all, there is no such thing as a purely English house. It would have been filled with objects brought back from the Grand Tour, a few French antiques and, of course, some Italian. This library is about the whole idea of connoisseurship—a very strong-willed connoisseur, like John Malkovich in *Portrait of a Lady*, whose palazzo in Florence was filled with rare and precious objects. This is the room of someone who has complete and utter confidence in his own taste.

I liked the dark walnut paneling that was already in the room, and decided to set it off with insets of fabric—a green-blue ikat that I had woven in Thailand. Why ikat? Because it's primitive and subtle. The wood was a little stiff, and I wanted to loosen it up. The ikat gives me a backdrop that pulls together all these dissimilar paintings and drawings—works by Picasso, Sonia Delaunay, David Bomberg. The mirror over the French marble mantel is English nineteenth-century, and instead of letting it stand alone, I hung various tiles around it—Hispano-Moroccan, Persian. They add to that sense of a collector's lair. Then I brought in Islamic pottery, Cambodian bronzes, Chinese cloisonné. The curtains are a saffron-colored Indian silk, embroidered by Lesage, the legendary Parisian company. In a room like this, you can get away with big, exotic gestures. Eccentricity thrives in England, where it's practically part of the national character. Think of Lord Leighton's house, with all those Moorish tiles on the walls.

Above: The Chinese altar table in the foreground has the kind of old, crackled finish I love. Two black Swedish urns and a blue-and-white Chinese bowl are set on top. If I'm going to buy a piece of blue-and-white porcelain, it has to be beautifully shaped and painted—and a little eccentric. This has an unusual pomegranate design. The objects in the center of the mantel are a Chinese cloisonné censer and two bronze Tibetan roundels.

Opposite: Three squares and a star add up to an intriguing composition. A seventeenth-century Persian tile is set on a Japanese chest. The paintings are by Picasso (top) and Franz Kline.

A Chinese altar table stands behind the sofa, which is covered in a printed velvet I designed, inspired by the pattern of an Indian carved window. The library is so large—one of the three original drawing rooms—that it made sense to have it double as a dining room. The English dining table from Ariane Dandois in Paris also functions as a library table, a place to gather books and papers.

The two guest rooms are comparatively small, but no less fantastic. One is full of Bloomsbury Group paintings, with yellow Fortuny fabric on the walls. The other began at a haute couture show. Funny how you get ideas. I was lucky enough to be invited to Christian Lacroix's show at the École des Beaux-Arts, and he sent the models out against a backdrop of these enormous black-and-white blowups of paintings. I loved that idea, and replicated it by wrapping this guest room in a grisaille wallpaper by Zuber, portraying Arcadian groves and temples all in shades of gray. The vistas expand the narrow space. Then I furnished it with a stately Neoclassical Russian secretaire and hung claret red curtains. The red is such a good clarifier, making the gray and white look even more crisp. It adds romance. It's regal.

The master suite had a 1930s Jean-Michel Frank

Left: In this guest room, the grisaille wallpaper by Zuber sets the tone, and the daybed is done in the same handsome grays. It was modeled after a Louis XVI original and made for me by Frederick P. Victoria & Son.

Above: The Russian secretary dates from the 1830s and is made with the most beautifully figured woods. Claret red curtains are that one exhilarating burst of color in a very serene room, which seems infinitely larger thanks to the panoramic wallpaper.

Pages 147–48: In the master bedroom, the wall behind the bed is covered in squares of parchment and, picking up on the 1930s theme, the bed is covered in shagreen. The curtains at the floor-to-ceiling windows are made in two layers—winter-white cashmere with blue-green sheers underneath. The starburst mirror was probably made in the 1950s by Line Vautrin, a French sculptor and jeweler whose work is highly prized today.

kind of look, with parchment already on the walls, so I went with that idea. I made a sleigh bed out of shagreen. It's hard enough to find a small box in real shagreen. Who in their right mind would ever make a bed out of it? Yet it's possible, and it has this extraordinary pale blue-gray color. Then I set two Ruhlmann-esque night tables beside it, with tops made of crushed eggshells set into lacquer. Frank is rather easy to translate into a modern aesthetic because his furniture was so geometric. But Émile-Jacques Ruhlmann was more adventurous, and his furniture was even more beautifully made—often with eggshell lacquer by Jean Dunand. What could be more odd? We throw away eggshells without a thought, but put them in lacquer and suddenly they're the most rare and incredible thing. I think there were two great zeniths of craftsmanship in France, the first in the eighteenth century and the second in the 1920s and 1930s. Some people argue that the furniture of Ruhlmann surpasses the furniture of the court at Versailles. Human beings have always been obsessed with the richness and rarity of materials, whether it's Russia's fabled Amber Room or Frank Gehry's titanium.

I love shagreen, malachite, mica, parchment, and leather. Any material becomes more interesting once you take it out of its expected context. Everyone wears leather shoes, but the minute you do a floor of leather squares, it feels so much richer. There are certain materials that are so magical that they alter your perception of space—like handpainted wallpaper or even the cheapest mirror. They can hit you in a place that's beyond logic. Parchment is one of those materials, so of course I kept it in this bedroom. I bought a pretty silverleafed chest from a house Frances Elkins did in Chicago and hung Venetian mirrors and Irving Penn photographs of flowers. There's a sitting area in front of the fireplace with big comfortable chairs upholstered in a beautiful Clarence House linen, woven in pale blue with abstract white cherry blossoms. Wherever the walls weren't lined with parchment, I covered them in celadon silk, so the room was all pale greens and blues and shimmery silver.

This apartment is an extraordinary space filled with extraordinarily beautiful objects. It has real character and weight, and what I mean by that is not a heaviness but a solidity, so the house and the location, the architecture and the furnishings feel equally monumental—and interconnected. I was after an unusual juxtaposition of objects, chosen with a connoisseur's eye. I wanted to make a home worthy of my very discerning clients.

After all, life is fleeting. All these objects are eventually going to go back into the mix. The only thing that differentiates you from the rest of the pack is how you put them together while you have them.

Pages 149–50: The 1920s and 1930s were the height of glamour in London. For me, the silver-leafed chest by Frances Elkins, the Venetian mirror, and the mirrored stool seem to embody that era. Along with the silver frames on the Irving Penn photographs, they also capture and reflect the light from the windows on the opposite wall.

Opposite: The breakfast table feels like something you might see on a chic boat. I couldn't resist adding a flash of exuberance with a sunburst mirror, originally made in the seventeenth century and regilded in the 1950s. The photograph is by Robert Polidori. The painted wallpaper was custom-made by Elizabeth Dow.

Above: When my clients bought the apartment, the kitchen had already been redone with Bulthaup cabinets and gray granite. It looked great, but perhaps a bit cold. A window seat catches the morning light and helps warm things up.

MARTHA'S VINEYARD, MASSACHUSETTS

There are certain things that are hard to beat. Today, I had a grilled kosher hot dog for lunch. You could have fancier food, but sometimes there's nothing better than simplicity. The same principle applies to this old-fashioned beach house on Martha's Vineyard, designed for longtime clients who love the Vineyard and have been going there for thirty years. They found a dazzling site on a bluff overlooking the ocean in a land cooperative that was put together in the 1920s. The roads are unpaved; there's a real sense of nature.

In the last ten years, most of the houses that have been built in almost every beach community in America are East Hampton houses—what I call Martha-by-mail houses.

The image of the Hamptons beach house in movies

has become the standard, but it's not actually appropriate everywhere. Here, Oscar Shamamian and I wanted to really try and get the essence of the Vineyard, which is a lot simpler and more Yankee sea captain in a way. There are big whaling houses in Edgartown, but the Vineyard never had that robber-baron tradition of faux-Normandy mansions or the pretty English country house at the beach.

Instead, we were thinking of the island's fishing shacks. We wanted a house that looked more like a camp than a resort, because when you go to visit these clients, it really is like summer camp for grown-ups. First they haul you off on these long, long bike rides, or a hike, or kayaking, or canoeing. Then you're handed a pail and sent out to pick blueberries for lunch. By this time you're

Above: The Shingle-style house, designed by Oscar Shamamian, is not one big, regular form. It's broken up into a group of modestly scaled wings, to make it look as if they had been added on at different times. It should weather well—the green paint on the trim already blends into the landscape. Instead of laying a nice, tight path, we scattered the flagstones irregularly and let the grass grow in between.   Scott Frances / *Architectural Digest* © Condé Nast Publications Inc.

Opposite: Everyone gravitates to the screened porch—a breezy place to sit in summer with a beautiful view of the ocean. The walls at either end—one has a fireplace—are puzzled together with fieldstone. I love those antique train-station lights and the comfortable wicker furniture.
Scott Frances / *Architectural Digest* © Condé Nast Publications Inc.

Pages 155–56: The entrance hall, which opens to the living room, has a Yankee sensibility. I bought the old grain-painted door, which is now on a closet, and that Windsor settee because they have that plain and useful early American simplicity, which is so beautiful to me. The old architectural finial standing by the front door could be a piece of sculpture.

desperate for a swim, and they march you right over to the freezing ocean. They refuse to have anything so suburban as a heated pool. They didn't even want to put in air conditioning.

The big thing was: How do we fit all this life—a program for a family with three grown children and guests—into a 4,500-square-foot envelope with strict height restrictions? The covenants of the co-op were written to ensure that no houses on its 2,000 acres could be seen from the others. That meant we couldn't have two full floors, so Oscar designed a classic Shingle-style house with dormer windows close to the rooflines. It doesn't read like a big house, more like a little house that has been added on to over the years. Very low-key, with a screened porch at one end. We did some research and looked at traditional colors. The shingles on the outside of the house will weather to gray and the trim is painted a dull green, unlike the white trim of a Nantucket house. Houses here have a picnic bench–like solidity.

When you enter, you walk through a low, narrow hall that looks over the living room, which is a step down. Coming in low increases the illusion of height in the living room beyond, and without any walls or barriers, you get a sweep of space and a view straight out to the ocean. The height change from the entry into the living room also delineates the difference between the two spaces. There's a simple staircase just to the left of the front door.

When it comes to country style, there's Connecticut Country, which I think of as Greenwich or East Hampton. And there's Gentleman Country, which is the American version of the English country house. And then there's what I call Dirt Country, which is more about a sense of austerity. It's antique black and rust and dark green tables and settees and grain-painted chests. It's almost sculptural in its simplicity. We're not talking gilded frames, elaborate Chinese export porcelain, or Duncan Phyfe chairs. This is more severe. I bought a lot of pieces from the Bill Blass sale—big terra cotta jugs, old maps, Wedgwood, and wooden pitchers. There's a little folk art, an old Windsor chair with some of its original black paint.

In the living room, which is not very big, there's a lot of very comfortable upholstery. These people do not go out to dinner every night. They're going to spend a lot of time at home, with their guests. So there are plenty of chairs and sofas gathered around the fireplace. And a window seat. All covered in woven hemp, which has this lovely gray, oyster-like color that seems so appropriate for the Vineyard. There are big wooden tables for playing Scrabble or doing a puzzle. No TV. It's the kind of room where you'd be perfectly comfortable taking a nap on the sofa at 4 o'clock in the afternoon. Then, if guests are coming to dinner, all you have to do is put some road-stand flowers into those jugs and light a few candles.

The living room opens onto the dining room, which has a dining table at one end and a fireplace, with a sofa and chairs at the other. When they need more space, they just move the sofa and expand the table, but otherwise it makes for a very cozy, informal dining space. When it's cold outside, they can just live in here, and the kitchen. It's really a house within a house.

The kitchen is one of my favorite rooms. Unlike a lot of people, including myself, the clients cook, and the kitchen is a big part of their life. We painted it in Charleston green and black and khaki, early American colors, which makes it a little dark and somber. I wanted to do something that was the polar opposite of the typical white-marble, white-cabinet Hamptons kitchen. This is a little tougher and more rigorous. It's also a nice retreat from the bright white light of summer.

My clients were very patient, and they indulged my complete obsession with ship paintings from the eighteenth and nineteenth centuries. I've always liked paintings that are about movement—volcano paintings, campfire paintings. I'm less attracted to still lifes. A boat picture is moving, with the waves crashing and the sails billowing. Things that imply movement really give a room and a house a sense of energy and life. The East Coast idea of whaling and shipping, the mystery and adventure of being at sea—it all connects to the real history of the place. It's part of trying to create an ambience for the house, as though it were originally built by or for someone whose livelihood depends on ships.

Because of the size and height limitations of the house, getting in the four bedrooms upstairs under the dormers, and a guest room downstairs, and a small guesthouse and tiny library, was a tough act of geometry.

Pages 157–58: Look at the graceful, scrolling curves of the nineteenth-century settee in the living room, and then compare it to the straightforward lines of that American tavern table, with the horse weathervane on top. These early craftsmen have a lot to teach us about shape and proportion. The wood pieces add a little backbone to all the cozy upholstery. I love the curlicue back of that armchair by the fireplace.

Opposite: I had a set of chairs made for the dining room and upholstered them in the same creamy hemp I used in the living room, to keep it really spare. The table is set with copies of eighteenth-century Chinese export porcelain—dishes that feel right for the house and can be used every day. The jug, which used to belong to Bill Blass, is filled with Queen Anne's Lace and other field flowers. Scott Frances / *Architectural Digest* © Condé Nast Publications Inc.

Pages 161–62: Instead of the typical bright white kitchen, I wanted something that felt more like the Vineyard, in earthy, natural colors like green and taupe. The upper cabinets have old-fashioned sliding glass doors. The countertops are made of Lagos Azul limestone. I modeled the island after a nineteenth-century table and kept it clean—no sink or cooktop—so it would look more like a piece of furniture. Scott Frances / *Architectural Digest* © Condé Nast Publications Inc.

The master bedroom is very simple, with a big fireplace surrounded by pretty antique Delft tile. There's a deep, comfortable window seat overlooking the water to lounge in for a long read, and a tiger-maple cannonball bed. In the master bath, there's a clawfoot tub with another view of the water. The marble is a shadowy gray, not that bright white. I think it's nice to come back to something that feels soft and grounded after a long, sunny day at the beach. Throwing down a wet towel or having a dog sleep at your feet is not going to ruin anything in these rooms.

In the library, the husband wanted the ceiling to feel like the inside of a boat, as if a hull had been turned upside down on top of you. It's a beautifully waxed mahogany, and the walls are also paneled in wood. There's a big sofa upholstered in linen velvet, and a Georgian leather-topped desk in a big bay window that looks out to sea. At night, with a fire in the fireplace, it's especially beautiful.

A lot of people who had lived in the community forever were very interested in the goings-on as we were building the house—as any neighbors would be. When we were unloading the furniture, one woman came over to me and said, "Oh, it's so nice to see such lovely family things going into the house." Little did she know these things had all been acquired so recently. To me, the greatest compliment was that the house clearly already had a real sense of history, and a real sense of family.

Above: The master bedroom is small and cozy, just as it would have been in the old days, and very shipshape. There's a cupboard tucked into that low corner and a window seat in the dormer—a great place to read. The Delft tiles around the fireplace make it feel special. Of course, I had to hang one of my favorite ship paintings over the mantel. Scott Frances / *Architectural Digest* © Condé Nast Publications Inc.

Opposite: In a guest bedroom, an antique fanlight hangs over the pencil-post bed and echoes the windows of the house. Beadboard gives the walls a spare, almost nautical austerity. I like the way architect Oscar Shamamian ran it in different directions, which feels fresh and almost modern. That's a fine Windsor chair, with its original paint. Scott Frances / *Architectural Digest* © Condé Nast Publications Inc.

Pages 165–66: In the bathroom, you have a view of the ocean from the antique refurbished tub. There's a vintage rolling doctor's cart for bath salts and towels. Once again, I used those old drabware colors—khaki and tan and tobacco—which temper the light so the room feels steeped in a sense of age. Yet when it's overcast and foggy, the warmth in the colors comes out. There's nothing frivolous about this room. It has a kind of Andrew Wyeth severity.

Pages 167–68: This charming little guesthouse sits all by itself on the property. Some of the furniture is old, like that tall French leather chair and the painted blanket chest. Some is new, like the bed, although it's made the old-fashioned way. An American landscape painting hangs over the headboard. The simple Roman shades are made of a Rogers & Goffigon ticking stripe.

SANTA YNEZ, CALIFORNIA

This house had sat empty for twenty years when my clients saw it and decided to buy it because it reminded them of Italy. It's in the Santa Ynez Valley, just north of Santa Barbara, and has a view of rolling hills and trees. If you stand outside and squint, you could be in Tuscany.

The house was just a shell, and the idea was to turn it into this incredibly beautiful Italian villa. I'm not a big believer in creating something that's not there, but this particular fantasy worked with the massing of the house—a main center-hall structure with two flanking wings—and

its surroundings. Then the clients helped the illusion along by planting a vineyard, as well as laurel, cedars, and Italian cypress trees.

The entrance hall was this vast empty space, forty feet high, which constitutes a big chunk of the house. It was important that it set a tone, evoking the grace and ease of a Italian country house that has been lived in for generations. Architect Mark Rios and I conceived of the hall as an interior courtyard. We covered the walls with Venetian plaster and laid a stone floor. We reworked the

Above: Imagine sitting under this pergola with a glass of wine and looking out at the Santa Ynez Valley. It reminded my clients of Tuscany, so they planted their own vineyard and dug a lake, to help with irrigation. The wrought iron furniture by Janus et Cie is covered in burgundy Sunbrella fabric.

Opposite: The scale of the entrance hall is huge and the furniture had to be equally massive to hold its own in the forty-foot-high space. I think that Italian pedestal table in the center of the room is seven feet across. I was thrilled when I spotted the Medici shield in Florence because I knew I needed something large and dramatic for that wall. The iron chandelier is by Rose Tarlow.

staircase and added classical columns. Lanterns, very softly lit, hang all around the perimeter and give it the feeling of a cloister.

The strength of the design is derived from its scale and simplicity, and the furnishings had to have a similar monumental quality. The clients and I made seven trips to Italy, shopping in small towns and big cities and eating all these fabulous meals on the way. We covered Lucca, Parma, Bologna, Venice, and Florence. We went everywhere from country fairs to the finest antiques dealers. We were at the antiques fair in Parma by 6:00 AM and bought a container's worth of objects, including that seventeeth-century Northern Italian chest by the stairs. On top of it, I arranged an eccentric collection of old specimen marble balls. That huge Italian Biedermeier table in the center of the entrance hall was bought at auction and turned out to be the perfect size to anchor the space.

The rooms were big and they needed to have spirit and charm so they didn't feel too solemn and museum-like. In the sunroom, which is really the family room, we did it with color. The fiery reds make it feel lush in summer and warm in winter, as if you have all this light and energy coming from within the space. The sofa is covered in this lovely Pierre Frey fabric, with thick bullion fringe. For me, there's just something too suburban about plain fabric sofa skirts. The pillows are mismatched and piled on, but not so many that they push you off. The mantel is probably French, maybe Italian, and on top of it are all these eighteenth-century French and Italian storage jars that we also bought in Parma. We found a collection of Sicilian tile, framed it and hung it on the walls, next to these dark Italian portraits. All these exotic elements seem to have been gathered over time. Nothing feels too planned. The room is held together by pattern and texture. Individual pieces may catch your eye but they all vibrate at the same level, which makes it work.

The living room is more pale and reductive. A dark linen velvet sofa and a black-and-gold Florentine mirror keep it from floating away. In this very symmetrical

Deep rich reds and ochres give the sunroom a glow even on a cloudy day. The sofa is upholstered in L'Incourt by Pierre Frey and the chairs in a nubby wool from Cowtan & Tout. Even the coffee table brings in a little more color and pattern with its specimen marble top. The faux-bois painted cabinet to the left of the fireplace hides a TV.

Opposite: Volcano paintings have been popular for centuries—a take-home memento for Englishmen visiting Pompeii on the Grand Tour. Here, I hung a collection above a Sicilian chest with a faux-marble painted top.

Above: The black Florentine mirror above the fireplace is like a low note in a piece of music. Its darkness balances out the lighter top notes in the living room. The nineteenth-century silvered brass candlesticks and the eighteenth-century bust on the mantel are from J. F. Chen. I covered the custom-made sofa in Concord linen velvet from Nancy Corzine. The eighteenth-century slat-backed armchair is upholstered in Rigata Veronese from Clarence House.

house, the dining room and the library are in the same position in opposite wings, so it was important that they relate to each other. Both have dark coffered ceilings and dark wooden furniture. The dining room is my version of a convent dining room, with a beautiful Florentine sideboard and a table in antique wood that was made for the space. The big comfortable leather chairs have been aged as well. It all gives the room a slightly monastic look, but then the damask curtains and the vanilla walls turn golden in the candlelight—very romantic.

A pool table takes the stuffiness out of the library. The walls are lined with glass-fronted cabinets that hold books and give it a collector's sensibility. When it's ninety-five degrees outside, you can close the curtains and create this green cocoon that feels perfectly cool and contained.

In the master bedroom, I used a fabric that I like a lot—Bennison's Hibiscus linen—on the sofa and chairs. It has that tea-dyed look and a palette of russet red and olive that fits the mood of the house. The bed is very large—a California king—so I set it into a niche framed in tailored linen curtains to break it down a bit. I had the four-posters modeled after a bed in the papal collection, and their height acts as a counterpoint to that huge, king-sized horizontal surface. The eighteenth-century apothecary cabinets, used to hold books, add a little masculine edge, to balance out the florals on the furniture. The room opens onto a loggia that overlooks the lake and the vineyards. I furnished it with American wicker with old leather cushions, a set I bought back East. It's cozy, and reminds me of something Renzo Mongiardino would do. No matter how grand the room, he will always have

I prefer rooms that give you more than one reason to come inside, like this library that also houses a pool table. The pendant lights above it are from Reborn Antiques. The curtains are Rogers & Goffigon's Shaker linen in Camp. They just break on the floor with a few inches of extra fabric, which adds to the old-world atmosphere. The rug is an eighteenth-century Turkish Oushak.

Above: The dining room is the simplest room in the house, in a way—just dark wood against light walls—and yet somehow it feels grand. Perhaps it's the coffered ceiling or the candlelit antique Venetian glass chandelier. I had the table custom-made and upholstered the chairs in AH Savage leather form Ashbury Hides. The Ghiordes rug dates from 1850. The linen damask curtains are from Brunschwig & Fils.

Opposite: We brought a few antiques into the kitchen so it doesn't look completely new. The breakfast table is eighteenth-century Italian. I found the chairs in Florence and bought them for their beautifully shaped back. They're slipcovered in a simple cotton check. Architect Mark Rios built that giant wood cabinet to divide the space, creating a butler's pantry on the other side. It also houses the refrigerator unobtrusively.

something like an inexpensive Indian cotton or a simple wicker chair—something that lets you breathe a bit.

Mongiardino was a master of theatricality, but there was nothing false about it. His rooms never look like a set. They always feel inhabited. I want my rooms to have that same sense of comfort and ease, which traditionally comes only with time. Decorating, for me, is a bit like knitting a sweater for someone you know, who's hopefully going to love it and wear it and inhabit it. Each room is created with the character of the clients in mind and a sense of the place it's going to be. You're designing in anticipation of the life to come. And it will all happen very naturally, if you've given people what they need.

A chaise is one of the most inviting pieces of furniture you can own. This one in the master bedroom is upholstered in one of my favorite linen prints—Bennison's Hibiscus. The curtains are made of Frederica Plain linen in Cream from Nancy Corzine and trimmed with brown braid. The eighteenth-century walnut cabinets are from the Gerard Conte Gallery in Paris.

The guest bedroom is furnished with a pretty Italian bed. The sofa at the foot of it is covered in a woven stripe. By creating a comfortable sitting area, I turned a single room into a virtual suite. It's lovely to sit there and look out at the lake.

ENCINAL BLUFF, CALIFORNIA

My clients were looking for a place in Malibu and there happened to be a very prominent house for sale. It was huge—19,000 square feet. Very 1980s, with no real detail, but it was on an extraordinary piece of land. The lot next door was also available, so they could combine the two into nearly twelve acres with its own private beach.

An amazing property, but clearly we had to rethink the house. I said, "Let's go to the Veneto and look at houses by Palladio." We walked through the Villa Foscari, better known as La Malcontenta, and the Villa Capra, known as La Rotonda, and we loved the way those rooms felt—airy, spacious, very simple and severe. Perfect for the beach. These villas were actually built in the sixteenth century as summer houses for noble Venetian families. The furnishings were relatively spare. The rooms were not overadorned. It was more about beautiful volumes, open to the breeze. The expansiveness and the spareness

---

Above: The tall columns on the rear façade accentuate the verticality of the house, built on a cliff top in Malibu overlooking the Pacific Ocean. Oscar Shamamian was dreaming of Palladio when he designed it. The center section, topped by a pediment, is flanked by two wings. The water in the backyard pool is level with the ground, so it looks almost natural.

Opposite: The front door is carved out of walnut and based on a Palladian original. All the steps, the terracing, and the interior flooring are made from pietra serena, which we picked out ourselves at a quarry outside Florence. I had the lanterns made in England. The pots are planted with boxwood and lavender.

This loggia is equipped with a seventeenth-century Tuscan fireplace. The two sofas flanking it are made of woven rope and based on an original designed in France back in the 1930s or 1940s. The round table was made by Soane in London and the T-shaped chairs surrounding it are copies of chairs that were originally designed for Palladio's Villa Malcontenta near Venice. There is no color here other than what is integral to the materials.

Opposite: The play of light and shadow in this hallway makes me think of Vermeer. A seventeenth-century stone bowl is set on a Chinese puzzle table purchased at Grusenmeyer in Ghent. The early eighteenth-century hall chair still has its original leather. Then there is that beautiful Elizabethan portrait, painted on wood. It's incredibly dark and dramatic. The mysterious, shadowy quality of this hall has the effect of making the sunroom just beyond feel even brighter.

Above: Looking in the other direction, you see two nineteenth-century copies of Roman stools under a Michael Goldberg painting from the 1960s. The Chinese root table in the distance was found at Jean-Claude Ciancimino in London. This enfilade, with the doors aligned so you can see all the way to the end, is one of Palladio's architectural signatures.

led to a new concept for the Malibu house—sixteenth-century loft living.

Oscar Shamamian and I took the existing house down to the studs and tore off 3,000 square feet to improve the massing and make a perfectly symmetrical facade. We played up the height and the size, enlarging doorways and reinforcing axes and generally trimming it up to Palladian proportions. The house had been laden with crystal chandeliers and elaborate curtains, but that's not how I think of the beach. This reinvention was more

about space and light and land. To have this kind of acreage in Los Angeles is very unusual. Visitors drive into what looks like a park. At the end of an allée of trees, you come upon this large stucco and stone-edged house, very severe. Huge industrial-scale bronze-and-glass windows open in back to a wide expanse of grass on a cliff that drops off to the ocean.

It's an incredibly dramatic site, and we wanted you to feel the impact as soon as you step into the house. You walk into a double-height entrance hall and your

Opposite: I bought that seventeenth-century Persian carpet thinking I would eventually cut it in two, but it turned out to be just the right size for this large living room. There are two seating groups, focused around a fireplace at each end. I had a hemp fabric custom-woven for the sofas. The palette is pale, except for the indigo in the rug and the red fabric on the two Georgian chairs, which I had copied from an antique Indian textile.

Above: On the bamboo coffee table, there are three bronze Japanese koi, a Chinese vessel, and a Japanese tray inlaid with porcelain. I like all the different shapes and textures. The flowers in the vase are arranged just as casually. I don't want any stiffness in my rooms.

eye is immediately pulled out through the living room straight ahead to the ocean. The proportions of these rooms are so commanding and strong that they would be beautiful even without anything in them. As in Palladio's villas, the materials are incredibly raw, yet refined. I decided that the entire ground floor would be paved in pietra serena, the stone they used to construct the city of Florence. We traveled to the quarry in Italy and picked out the slabs we wanted. Upstairs, the floors are reclaimed French and Italian oak—just waxed, not varnished. The walls are Venetian plaster—no flat surfaces, everything has texture and dimension. The plaster seems to sculpt the space. It absorbs light in an old-world way and changes color from room to room, all basically variations on the color of the sand on the beach below. Bleached walnut doors have a sun-faded quality.

Above: In the Chinese scholar's bookcase, I've created a landscape of objects—some Chinese, some African, some Cambodian. It's a study in dark and light, shape and texture.

Right: Once again, I've used a large table between the two seating groups in the living room to anchor the space and mark a passageway through the center. The mirror over the fireplace is seventeenth-century Dutch. The coffee table in the foreground is from Axel Vervoordt. Bill Blass once owned that Egyptian Revival chair, and I liked it so much that I made a copy of it for my own entrance hall.

The living room is very long, with a fireplace at each end. One is a sixteenth-century Florentine chimneypiece and the other is its copy. The big square mirrors that hang above them are probably seventeenth-century Dutch. I bought them from a Spanish dealer at the Maastricht art fair. The Persian carpet is something I found ages ago, old and rare and scaled perfectly to the room—one of those serendipitous miracles that sometimes happens in decorating. There are two seating groups with big comfortable sofas and chairs, each oriented around a fireplace. I had this antique Indian textile and thought it would look beautiful on a pair of Georgian armchairs that once belonged to Katherine Graham, so I had it copied by Rossi in Italy. They basically Xeroxed it and then had it digitally printed on linen, which gives it an unusual quality. Then there are a number of Asian things—a pair of Chinese scholar's bookcases, very tall. A life-size Ghandaran figure, sculpted in stone, stands in a window.

This house has such extraordinary light from the shifting colors of the sky and the ocean. Often when I have things finished in

The sunroom has industrial-size steel-and-glass doors and a glass roof that retracts at the push of a button. With the doors open and the roof out of sight, the room becomes a modern-day version of a Roman atrium, open to the breeze. The sofa is covered in a stripe I designed for Cowtan & Tout. The chairs are covered in a Belgian linen that I had custom-dyed to get that particular purple. I used Moroccan textiles to make the pillows.

The sitting room in the guest wing represents a blend of many cultures. The eighteenth-century door surrounds are English, found at Jamb in London. Jamb also made the Georgian-style fireplace for me. Then there's an English mirror, an Italian chandelier from Amy Perlin, a Swedish klismos chair, and a Syrian inlaid table. The sofa is covered in a paisley I designed for Jasper, the pillows are made from African textiles, and the rug is actually a Navajo blanket.

advance, such as wood pieces that aren't antique, I find that the finishes are not quite right when I bring them in. I have to redo them on-site, because the light has such a specific color and clarity. I remember a movie with Isabelle Adjani called *Camille Claudel*, the story of a woman sculptor who studied with Auguste Rodin and fell madly in love with him. The colors in that movie are all taupes and grays and pale blues. For this house, I was into an oyster gray, the color of the beach on a misty, foggy morning. That's the color of the stone on the floor. Then there's lots of cream and off-white, as well as Roman colors like terra cotta, faded marigold, pale burgundy, and indigo. All the linen for the curtains has been washed first, so it falls very softly.

The library and dining room, on opposite sides of the living room, are mirror images of each other, and I used the same burnt-red linen for the curtains in each room. Both ceilings are coffered in wood, with a raw, wire-brushed finish. The wood puts a lid on each room so it becomes more intimate, like a pair of beautiful boxes. Two eighteenth-century Flemish

Left: The library is a cozy, after-dinner room where you can watch TV or read. We made the etageres out of steel and antique walnut. The linen curtains are Pompeian red, a color with an almost primitive appeal. The two campaign stools bring in another touch of Greco-Roman style.

Above: A study off the master suite has oak-paneled walls painted a driftwood color. The bookcase is a very severe English piece with stately home proportions. I bought the Georgian chair at a Sotheby's auction. An antique Japanese dining table is the perfect height for coffee.

chandeliers made of solid brass—they must weigh 175 pounds each—hang in the dining room and are lit with candles. Very splendid, but then the floor is covered in simple apple matting. The dining table is made from old bog-wood, which has a texture and feel to the grain that you don't get in ordinary wood. Made in the style of a seventeenth-century refectory table, it's very plain, just two big boards fourteen feet long. The chairs are Georgian, and some are antique. The others were handmade by a craftsman in England who took months to carve them, one at a time, out of heavy mahogany. Then I threw in a Chinese table and a pair of Japanese paper lanterns that sit on the floor.

Nothing I do is pure, and I love to play on that idea of dissonance. You can see it most clearly in the kitchen. Someone once gave me a book on feudal Japanese palaces, and I've been carrying around those pictures in my head. Then I crossed that idea with a northern European castle (creamy plaster walls, wood beams) and modern minimalism to get this fusion of Japanese tonsu chests and stainless steel. The cabinetry is made of elm, very simple and severe. No visible clutter. Everything is hidden behind doors. It's *Shogun* in Malibu.

Above: There's a pleasing symmetry to this composition, made up of an English mirror over an Italian console—each one of a pair. And then I threw in a Japanese lantern, which is the unexpected object that shakes it up a bit.

Right: The dining room belongs in a Rembrandt painting, with that long table and those huge eighteenth-century brass chandeliers. The table was made for me out of old bogwood by Kevin Brown in California. Will Fisher at Jamb in London was able to duplicate the original Georgian chairs, so we could have a larger set. The cupboard with the extraordinary oyster veneer—made of slices of trees—was originally owned by Bill Blass.

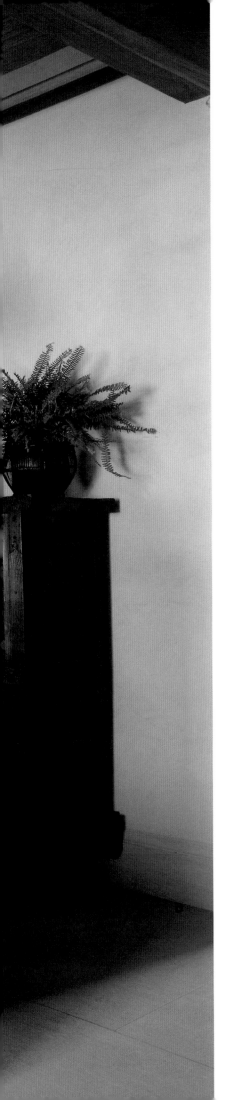

Left: This is my twenty-first-century Japanese feudal kitchen, which is one of my favorite rooms in the house. Materials are used in a way that feels very sculptural. The island is made of walnut over stainless steel, with an inset of stone around the sink. Next to it is a Japanese tonsu that dates back to the eighteenth century. The hanging lamps are made of fabric over a wood frame and were salvaged from a 1940s department store in Japan.

Above: A French farm table in the breakfast room is surrounded by English bobbin chairs, still covered in their original leather. I found the chairs at Colefax & Fowler. The cupboard is another purchase from the Bill Blass sale. The lantern is early nineteenth-century English.

The proportions are lofty. The ceiling in the kitchen must be twelve feet high, and the same is true of all the rooms upstairs. Each bedroom is unique. One is centered around a gracefully carved Florentine bed. In another, I had a campaign bed scaled up and made for me in India out of nickel silver. A headboard in a guest room is a slab of wood, by Nakashima. Everything has that handmade quality. You don't really need much else when you can see the grain in the wood, the carving on the stone. In this house, there is beauty in every element.

And the elements are slightly barbaric, as the French might say. The focus is on texture as much as technique. Old Master paintings hang next to primitive art and contemporary works by Sean Scully, David Smith, Philip Taaffe. I'm interested in the idea of a universal aesthetic that flows right through objects and periods. Is there a connection between a Franz Kline painting and an eighteenth-century Japanese table? When I put one of John Dickinson's vaguely Greco-Roman plaster tables next to a fragment of classical sculpture, I see a similarity of form. And then why not throw in a Nakashima headboard? Juxtaposing equally strong

Above: An Indian bed in a guest bedroom is made up with Moroccan pillows and a handwoven Swans Island wool blanket from Maine. The paintings on the wall are Japanese, bought at the Zen Gallery on the Left Bank in Paris. Everything in the room, including the antiques, is tied together by a contemporary sense of pattern.

Right: In another bedroom, an African shield hangs over the bed, which is covered in a Moroccan summer carpet I bought in Marrakech. The carpets are North African as well, made of straw and leather. The desk is nineteenth-century Japanese and the light fixture is an iconic piece by Serge Mouille that dates from the 1950s.

Opposite: Another guest room has a more European feel, with a canopy bed made of antique English bedposts. The pillows in front are covered with early American homespun shams. The mirrors are reproduction William Kent. The lanterns are Italian. A small Japanese table at the foot of the bed holds a selection of books—something no guest room should be without.

Above: The bed in the master suite was made for me by John Robshaw in India out of nickel silver. A Moroccan cotton carpet in a pale eggshell color doubles as a coverlet. Rather than grabbing all the attention with a big mirror or a major painting over the fireplace, I wanted people to focus on the early nineteenth-century Italian mantel as a work of art. So I kept the rest of the composition to a few still, quiet objects, like a small mother-of-pearl mirror and a stone plaque.

things from different cultures creates an intriguing rhythm. Somehow it feels profoundly humanist to bring them together.

Ancient and modern, high and low—I'm always mixing them up, and I don't care where an idea comes from. It could be inspired by an exhibit at the Metropolitan Museum of Art or a display at Target. The minute you become judgmental, you close off so many possibilities. There's a famously over-the-top movie called *Boom!* written by Tennessee Williams and starring Elizabeth Taylor and Richard Burton. Taylor lives in this incredible villa in Sardinia, bone-white and bleached by the sun. There's a scene where she walks through the house and servants follow behind her, shutting the curtains. I love the drama of all that white space. The house looks ancient and modern at the same time, which is one of the effects I was trying to achieve here. When I start working on a house, I basically comb through all the images I have filed away in my brain—it's like flipping through slides—until I find an idea that works. In one of the bedrooms upstairs, there's a paint line on the walls where the color of the Venetian plaster changes. It's two different shades, one on top and another on the bottom. That's taken from an Indiana Jones movie, where Harrison Ford is in a bar in Egypt and behind him there's a pale blue line. It's an incredibly beautiful image, and I've been holding it in my head for fifteen years. Finally, I got to use it.

Above: A nineteenth-century French chaise, covered in old purple wool, is set against a Japanese screen. The carpet is Chinese, the pillows are African, and the round stone object is Bactrian. But for me, what this vignette is really about is a kind of shimmer. It reminds me of those rooms in Venice where the light from the water is reflected on the ceiling and walls.

Right: Naturally, I had to have doors made to match the eighteenth-century door surrounds. Just outside this door is a nineteenth-century English commode made with seventeenth-century Japanese lacquered panels. The Wedgwood candlestick and oil lamp are made of black basalt. The vase is by Henry Dean, a Belgian glassmaker.

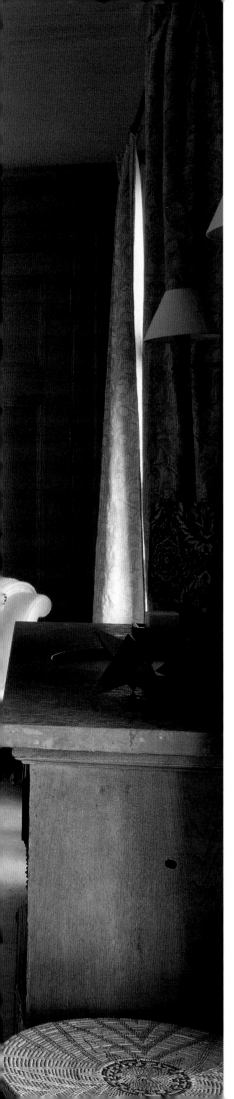

Left: Rusticated walls, designed by Oscar Shamamian, distinguish the husband's dressing room and bath. The closets are behind paneled doors, next to the English Regency chaise. The shower on the left is made of rare fossilized Derbyshire stone. The bronze dish lights are from Christopher Hodsoll in London.

Above: Looking the other way, you see an eighteenth-century Chinese cabinet and a Georgian armchair covered in hemp. An eighteenth-century table with a specimen marble top stands on a Greco-Roman mosaic inlay in the center of the room.

RESOURCES

MICHAEL S SMITH
DESIGNS

Agraria
Gump's of San Francisco
135 Post Street
San Francisco, CA 94108
Tel: 800-824-3632

Ann Sacks
8935 Beverly Boulevard
West Hollywood, CA 90069
Tel: 503-281-7751

Cowtan & Tout
979 Third Avenue,
Suite 1022/1005
New York, NY 10022
Tel: 212-753-4488

Kallista
8935 Beverly Boulevard
West Hollywood, CA 90069
Tel: 503-281-7751

Lowell
28 East 63rd Street
New York, NY 10065
Tel: 212-838-1400

Mansour Modern
8606 Melrose Avenue
West Hollywood, CA 90069
Tel: 310-652-1121

Patterson, Flynn & Martin
979 Third Avenue, Suite 632
New York, NY 10022
Tel: 212-759-5408

Samuel & Sons
Kneedler Fauchere
8687 Melrose Avenue,
Suite B600
Los Angeles, CA 90069
Tel: 310-855-1313

Shutters Hotel
1 Pico Boulevard
Santa Monica, CA 90405
Tel: 310-458-0030

Visual Comfort
Circa Lighting
2021 Bingle Road
Houston, TX 77055
Tel: 713-686-5999

ANTIQUES DEALERS AND
DESIGN RESOURCES

NEW YORK
Amy Perlin Antiques
206 East 61st Street, 4th Floor
New York, NY 10065

Ann-Morris Antiques
239 East 60th Street
New York, NY 10022
Tel: 212-755-3308

Beauvais Carpets
595 Madison Avenue,
3rd Floor
New York, NY 10022
Tel: 212-688-2265

H. M. Luther Antiques
61 East 11th Street
New York, NY 10003
Tel: 212-505-1485

John Robshaw Textiles
245 West 29th Street,
Suite 1501
New York, NY 10001
Tel: 212-594-6006

Niall Smith
306 East 61 Street, 5th Floor
New York, NY 10012
Tel: 212-750-3985

R. Louis Bofferding Fine Arts
121 East 71st Street
New York, NY 10021
Tel: 212-744-6725

Robert Altman LLC
306 East 61st Street,
3rd Floor
New York, NY 10065
Tel: 212-832-3490

CONNECTICUT
Michael Trapp
7 River Road
West Cornwall, CT 06796
Tel: 860-672-6098

LOS ANGELES
Collage Floral Design
3617 Eastham Drive
Culver City, CA 90232
Tel: 310-558-1300

Hollyhock
817 Hilldale Avenue
West Hollywood, CA 90069
Tel: 323-931-3400

Inner Gardens Incorporated
8925 Melrose Avenue,
Suite 146
Los Angeles, CA 90069
Tel: 310-274-0129

J. F. Chen Antiques
941 North Highland Avenue
Los Angeles, CA 90038
Tel: 323-655-6310

Lee Stanton Antiques
769 N. La Cienega Boulevard
West Hollywood, CA 90069
Tel: 310-855-9800

Paul Ferrante Incorporated
8464 Melrose Place
Los Angeles, CA 90069
Tel: 323-653-4142

Robert Kuo Limited
8686 Melrose Avenue
Los Angeles, CA 90069
Tel: 310-855-1555

R.M. Barohk Antiques
8481 Melrose Place
Los Angeles, CA 90069
Tel: 323-655-2771

LONDON
Blanchard
86/88 Pimlico Road
London, SW1W 8PL
Tel: 44-17-1823-6310

Ciancimino
85 Pimlico Road
London, SW1W 8PH
Tel: 44-20-7730-9959

Colefax and Fowler
110 Fulham Road
London, SW3 6HU
Tel: 44-20-7244-7427

De Gournay
112 Old Church Street
London, SW3 6EP
Tel: 44-20-7352-9988

Guinevere Antiques
574–580 Kings Road
London, SW6 2DY
Tel: 44-20-7736-2917

Hemisphere Decorative Art
173 Fulham Road
London, SW3 6JW
Tel: 44-20-7581-9800

Jamb, Ltd.
3 Dove Walk, Pimlico
London, SW1W8PS
Tel: 44-20-7736-3006

Westenholz Antiques Ltd
76–78 Pimlico Road
London, SW1W 8PL
Tel: 44-20-7824-8090

PARIS
Anne-Marie Monin
27, quai Votaire
75007 Paris
Tel: 33-1-49-26-90-40

Didier Aaron & Cie.
118, rue Faubourg
Saint-Honoré
75008 Paris
Tel: 33-1-47-42-47-34

Galerie Camoin Demachy
Buvelot S.A.
75007 Paris
Tel: 33-1-42-61-82-06

Perrin Antiquaires
98, rue du Faubourg
Saint Honoré
75008 Paris
Tel: 33-1-40-15-00-81

INDEX

ACKNOWLEDGMENTS

I would like to thank: Mark Matuszak, my talented friend and collaborator of fifteen years; Diane Dorrans Saeks for inspiring me to do books; Christine Pittel for her amazing ear and ability to capture my voice; Isabel Venero for making the book a reality; all the photographers and editors who have helped to capture what is an elusive craft; all the architects with whom I've worked, especially Oscar Shamamian, who always makes my work look smarter and better designed; James for being so patient; the undying support of Howard, Nancy, and Peggy, all of whom I forced to read countless drafts of my text; and, finally, all of my amazing clients and friends, without whose loyalty and trust none of this would have ever been possible.

PHOTOGRAPHY CREDITS

Courtesy of *ELLE DÉCOR*, Photography by Henry Bourne, styled by Margaret Russell
vi, 61–62, 107–18

Courtesy of *ELLE DÉCOR*, Photography by Simon Upton, styled by Cynthia Frank
40, 41–42, 43, 48, 49–50, 183–210

Grey Crawford
9, 19, 20, 74–78, 81

Brian Doben
57, 63, 64, 67–68

John Ellis
2, 30

Scott Frances
53–54, 71, 157–58, 165–66

Mark Matuszak
35, 47, 59–60, 65–66

Lisa Romerein
iv, 4, 5, 6, 7, 12, 16, 22, 27, 29, 32, 36, 44, 70, 84, 85, 86, 87–88, 89, 90, 91, 92, 93, 94, 119–130, 169–78, 179–80

Simon Upton
ii, x, 3, 10, 11, 13–14, 15, 21–22, 25–26, 27–28, 33–34, 37, 51, 55, 58, 95–106, 131–52

Simon Watson
52

First published in the United States in 2008 by
Rizzoli International Publications, Inc.
300 Park Avenue South
New York, NY 10010
www.rizzoliusa.com

Copyright © 2008 Michael S Smith

All rights reserved. No part of this publication may be reproduced, stored in a retrieval system, or transmitted in any form or by any means, electronic, mechanical, photocopying, recording, or otherwise, without consent of the publisher.

2008 2009 2010 2011 / 10 9 8 7 6 5 4 3 2 1

ISBN 13: 978-0-8478-3070-1

Library of Congress Control Number: 2008930944

Designed by Paul McKevitt for Subtitle

Printed in China